LET THERE BE UNITY OF RELIGIONS WITHIN DIVERSITY

THE WAY TO GO

by

ANTHONY M. LUONGO

"Behold how good and how pleasant it is for brethren to dwell together in Unity"

Psalm 133.1

ADAMS PRESS
CHICAGO

Printed in the
United States of America

Paperback Edition $1.95   Clothbound $3.50

Distributed by
TRANS WORLD PUBLICATIONS
Box 42, Pratt P. O. Sta.
Brooklyn, N. Y. 11205

PREFACE

MAN WILL NEVER FIND PEACE TO THE EXTENT
WHERE WAR IS FOREVER BANISHED UNTIL HE UN-
DERSTANDS THAT THE SAME SPIRIT IN ANY ONE OF
US IS ALSO IN EVERYONE ELSE. EACH PERSON,
REGARDLESS OF HUMAN PARENTHOOD IS IN REAL-
ITY OUR BROTHER, AND WE ALL HAVE ONE COMMON
FATHER—GOD. THE ONLY LASTING AND CREATIVE
FORCE IS UNSELFISH LOVE. NO SACRIFICE IS TOO
GREAT IN DEFENSE OF THIS PRINCIPLE. THIS PRIN-
CIPLE FINDS EXPRESSION AND FULFILLMENT IN
"UNITY OF RELIGIONS WITHIN DIVERSITY." THE
BROTHERHOOD OF MAN UNDER THE FATHERHOOD
OF GOD CAN BE ACHIEVED THROUGH THE BROTHER-
HOOD OF THE MONOTHEISTIC RELIGIONS, AND THE
SUBSTITUTION OF FORCE WITH RULE BY LAW.

Anthony M. Luongo

To my brother
Doctor Vito Luongo, M.D., F.A.C.S.
A veritable living Saint

Contents

Foreword

"My son, forget not my laws
But let your heart keep my commandments;
For length of days, and years of life,
And peace, will they add to you.
Let not kindness and truth forsake you;
Bind them about your neck;
Write them upon the tablet of your heart;
So shall you find favor and good understanding;
IN ALL YOUR WAYS ACKNOWLEDGE HIM,
AND HE WILL DIRECT YOUR PATHS;"
BE NOT WISE IN YOUR OWN EYES."

Proverbs Chap. 3 1-7
Am. S. Version
(Revision by Author)

Man has made more progress in science within the last fifty years than heretofore. Man has spent years of research to eliminate friction in machines in order to make them more efficient and less costly to operate and maintain. He has made untold innovations and inventions that stagger the imagination. He has made great progress in the manufacture of usable goods. Medicine has made tremendous strides in eliminating diseases that were once the scourge of mankind. He has extended the life span of man. He now travels faster than sound and has brought our neighborhood to each other's doorstep. He is exploring space to untold heights.

In the field of human relations and in religions man has not appreciably progressed. Great work will be done by religion when the differences of each religion are artistically blended and woven into a beautiful fabric, each religion, however, keeping and maintaining its own individuality. All religions will then see their own beauty enhanced by the other religions.

Religions should work together as instruments of peace, truth, freedom and love. They will then become the heartbeat of humanity.

If this book helps, in any way, to bring Unity of Religions within diversity closer to realization, and a better understanding between the monotheistic religions, it will have been in the service of God, Country and Man.

CHAPTER I

Truth

Man's unending quest is to know more and more about his Creator. The road to God is by truth. The more we know about truth, the more we know about God. If one were to ask how can I find God, the answer is always, see, speak, use and respect the truth. The more one delves into truth, be it in the physical, mental or spiritual realm, the greater becomes one's wisdom. In the attainment of truth man lives a fuller, more complete and peaceful life. In order for man to continue to be creative, his quest must be always for the truth.

George Bernard Shaw once stated: "My way of joking is to tell the truth. It's the funniest joke in the world." The truth can be so amazing that it brings forth torrents of laughter when it is uttered. There is truth in the words of Shaw.

We have had various definitions as to what constitutes an atheist. The common definition is: An athiest is a person who does not believe in the existence of God. Does this definition mean much? What is your definition of God? It is surprising how the definition of God varies not only among persons but also among the various organized monotheistic religions. There is a tremendous variance among people as to the meaning of God, what is He, what does he do, what is He constituted of, where is

1

He located, what are His attributes, where does He stand in the universe, how do we know He exists, ad infinitum?

Another definition of an atheist which has some meaning is to the effect that "an atheist is a person without visible means of support." It properly signifies and has the connotation that the atheist lacks spiritual insight and values which are necessary for a balanced personality. The conflicts between the value of the visible versus the invisible are eternal. The invisible is greater than the visible. However, this definition does not fully satisfy the average person as a complete and understandable explanation.

Some people profess a great belief in God and in actuality are atheists. Their deeds belie their belief. Some religious sects appear to possess a great knowledge of God and still are atheistic in thinking and in action. WHEN IS A PERSON A TRUE ATHEIST? When the true definition was given to an executive of a large insurance company, (who was a member of the college fraternity, Phi Betta Kappa honor society of intellectuals) he burst into profound laughter. It appeared to write the words "Quod Est Demonstrandum" (that which has been proven) as enunciated by Shaw. Did we strike a plausible, believable and fairly correct answer?

AN ATHEIST IS A PERSON WHO DENIES THE TRUTH. A well known physician and English author, Arthur Lynch, stated that "The only atheism is the denial of the truth." A person who speaks, uses and pays homage to the truth is a theist. If the minister or the theologian denies the truth knowingly, he is not a theist. If the falsehood be a delusion, he is nevertheless a deluded theist. Where the falsehood is through ignorance, its teaching is harmful. When we are not sure of the truth, truth requires that we so state. If we are compelled to decide what and where is the truth, we are to use our faculties to the best of our ability to accept the truth from believable evidence free from bias and by the use of a good conscience. When we scrutinize truth as deeply as our talents and our capacities permit we see that TRUTH IS GOD. The more we correctly research truth the more we discover the attributes of God. Know more of the truth, and you will know more of God. Follow the truth and you walk with God. Pay homage to the truth and you serve God. Love the truth and you love God. Follow the truth and you find God, and thus are spiritually rich.

What are some of the characteristics of truth. Truth—

1. Liberates while lies enslave and degrade.

2. Is humble and self-demonstrative.

3. Is not confinable, or definable, its presence is everywhere.

4. Is consistent and cannot contradict itself.

5. Is constant, unchanging, dependable and stable.

6. Is divine law and cannot be made truth by man's legislation or fiat.

7. Has no substitute, brooks no compromise, is demanding and exacting.

8. Is creative, vibrant and beneficial. Gives one peace of mind.

9. Brings love, faith, strength, power and justice into reality.

10. Lights the correct way to go, it is true guidance. (The truth as enunciated by Jesus is a very good yardstick to measure truth itself.)

11. Propagates itself.

12. Is indestructible. It is the only foundation upon which all order and virtues rest.

13. Consoles and uplifts, has no favorites.

14. Brings joy and happiness.

15. Purifies, even though it may hurt at times.

GENERALLY, THE GREATEST OBSTACLE IN THE LEARNING OF TRUTH IS THE UNLEARNING OF UNTRUTHS.

The question often arises—Is there any justifiable deviation from the truth? The immortal words of Horace Mann give us the answer:

"You need not tell all the truth, unless to those who have a right to know it all. But let ALL YOU TELL BE THE TRUTH."

How ridiculous it is for mortals to lie. When we lie we weave a net that usually catches us in its clutches and places us in bondage. Lies have very short legs. They cannot travel far and must eventually fall. Lies cannot stand erect for they rest on a hollow and unstable base. To deny the truth is to separate oneself from God.

Very often in court trials, both sides resort to falsehoods or exaggerations, the latter of which is also a form of lying. In a recent actual experience in a pending law suit before one of our higher tribunals of justice, one of the attorneys for the defense stated to the Trial Judge in a loud and expressive manner "Judge, if the truth were known." "STOP," shouted the Judge, "If the truth were known, the plaintiff would be in jail, the defendant would be in jail and perhaps the judge would be there also." It is for this reason that the greatest burden of "Administrative Justice" is to determine what is the truth, who is telling the truth and wherein lies the whole truth. Truth is justice in action. It is not very often that all of the parties are honestly mistaken as to what actually occurred or as to what is the truth. Self interest usually colors the truth.

Before we make any statement of fact that is worthy of utterance, we should consider four basic essentials, they are

1. Is it the truth?

2. Is it the right time to say it?

3. Is it the right place to say it?

4. Is it loving—does it produce good results?
   (Wisdom and love are team-mates)

If there is any doubt as to any of these four essentials, it is far better that the words be not spoken. In such a case silence is truly golden. The words we say are a very important part of our actions. Speech is a form of action. Each word we say should, as in the words of Benjamin Franklin, be carefully carved before they are made to fall from one's lips. We should form the good habit of having noble thoughts and to speak only the truth as God gives us the wisdom to see the truth.

It is often believed that at times it is proper to say a "white lie." It is felt that saying the truth instead of a "white lie" will hurt rather than help the party involved. It is to be noted, in the basic essentials, that if saying the truth is not loving, does not produce good results, we should keep silent. There is no reasonable justification for a so called "white lie." Let us consider the case of a person who is seriously ill with a presently incurable disease or condition and which is believed to be terminal

in nature. Should the hopelessness of one's condition be explained
to the patient? The doctor, if he must talk, should always tell
the patient the truth. In such an event the patient should be
told that everything within the doctor's ability and knowledge
is being done and that the final outcome depends on our Creator.
The doctor should not play the role of a prophet. It is far better
to take the penalty, if any, of silence than to speak a lie. The
choice of silence belongs to the individual and where the law
compels disclosure, one has the right to remain silent and to take
with complete resignation any penalty that the law exacts for
the refusal to speak. Divine law is true law. Where one's silence
is predicated upon Divine Law, the person should so state for the
record and present every legal proposition in his favor to sustain
his right to silence. Man never need fear man's judgment regardless of the penalty. God's judgment is always perfect and
there is eternity together with His unfailing love—His great and
benevolent gifts to us.

TRUTH AND WISDOM decree that there be Unity of Religions within Diversity. Some writers and theologians use the
words "Unity in Diversity," "Unity amidst Diversity" and "Unity
without Uniformity." They all mean the same thing. It is Unity
without Sameness, unity with Difference. God made each person
a human being with his eternal spirit. Yet, no two people are
alike since the world began. Can we not emulate Him in this
respect and realize His basic unity within ourselves, and thus
truly achieve the brotherhood of man, which in its final essence
is simply the realization of truth?

Have the various religions ever analyzed the reasons why
they are terribly divided, and the effect and the significance of
these divisions? Why have men like Stalin, Lenin, Hitler, Karl
Marx, Nagel and many others achieved power or influence in
causing countless numbers of individuals into channels of atheistic thinking? Are religions truly serving God when they are so
badly divided in the one calling where all men should be united?

Is there not but one God? What has happened to the great commandments of love as enunciated by Jesus?

What happens to any family where the mother and father lack unity? *Show me the family where there is discord and we will probably see a family where God is absent and the children generally suffer permanent scars and hardship the rest of their lives*—all as the result of disunity. Can one deny the truth in the statement that "the greatest human inheritance anyone can receive is to be the beneficiary of the unity and the love that one's parents have for each other."? If this is false then this entire writing is void of any meaning or significance and is but idle chatter. If money is the greatest of all inheritances in life, then we are worshiping the "golden calf." Are some religions worshiping the golden calf or is their worship one of Truth, Unity, Love, Justice, all of which are attributes of God?

Divisions of religions have created discord so that it has become axiomatic to warn:—"Do not discuss religion." Religions have so vastly created hatred among themselves that we find that there is no greater hatred than religious hatred, no bloodier war than religious wars, no greater division than religious division. Is it not time for us to correct this error? The power of correction lies within the realm of man.

Let us note the effect of divisions of religions upon couples of different denominations or sects that contemplate marriage. Clergymen warn the members of their congregation not to marry one of a different sect or faith. You will find this warning clearly expressed in their sermons, and writings of all types. This teaching has been so ingrained in individuals from generation to generation so that it causes disruption, disintegration and separation in most mixed marriages. Next to economic disputes, religious differences become the second important cause for marital separation and inharmony. Why has such a harmful doctrine been inculcated into the individual mind? We all admire the mind of the child because of its purity and freedom from malice. We then take the clear water and begin to pour into it impurities.

WHY? Is it because we seek to keep our congregation intact and fear the inroads that other religions may make on ours? Does it have an economic purpose? Are we afraid of healthy and necessary competition? Must we inject poisons into the minds of those who come to us for guidance because of our own selfish, egotistical and insecure "spiritualism." Do we truly love, when we preach avoidance instead of unity? Under the present state of religious teaching, can any clergyman in good conscience advise any of his congregation to marry a member of another sect or religion, knowing the indoctrination of division that has been preached so long? It takes courage for couples to marry regardless of the difference of religion. Presently such a marriage will achieve greater harmony if the two can agree upon a third sect or religion that both can believe in.

Jean Paul Sartre, well known French writer, on October 22, 1964 refused to accept the Nobel Prize for literature. WHY? His literary-philosophic cult of existentialism as defined by Webster's dictionary is as follows:

> Existentialism (Noun) a literary-philosophic cult of nihilism and pessimism, popularized in France after World War II, chiefly by Jean-Paul Sartre; it holds that each man exists as an individual in a purposeless universe, and that he must oppose his hostile environment through the exercise of his free will.

He explains his philosophy by writing:

> "Man can will nothing unless he has first understood that he must count on no one but himself; that he is alone, abandoned on earth in the midst of his infinite responsibilities, without help, with no other aim than the one he sets himself, with no other destiny than the one he forges for himself on this earth."

In all his striving for truth, Sartre finds the cosmos without purpose. What has led a brilliant mind, capable of using words as a great artist, to use his talents to dull the minds of men with the untruth that life has no purpose, but that which man determines from beginning to end. What a sadistic philosophy! He denies the divine order existent in the universe. What has made him a spiritual pauper? Search deep into his experience and you will undoubtedly find a person who has been disillusioned with religion. Can we in truth say there is no justification for such an attitude? Has religion spread the wisdom and the love among mankind that it should do? Truth works with justice. Justice in action is love. Has man been just? Has religion performed the task that God would want His believers to follow? God is Unity, Peace, Contentment and Harmony. Have religions been the instruments of such Unity, Peace, Contentment and Harmony that spiritual law demands from them? Either we know some Divine Law or we are complete neophytes. Let us build character through religion BY EXAMPLE as Jesus did, so that it will stand out as the Light of the world. Man may then by the use of a greater acquisition of love make a greater breakthrough from the natural world into the spiritual world. The human mind can achieve this miracle of miracles and some day will accomplish this goal. In order to achieve this greater love, religion is now seeking and following truth and Unity, not by choice but because of necessity.

Man is now faced with the dilemma of the ages. Man has a future with untold beautiful prospects for a very happy life. The scientists have discovered nuclear power which gives man the use of unlimited power. Up to the present time, it has been utilized much more for possible human destruction than the great potential for good. Again man is given the choice—the choice between life and death, between good and evil! Which will he choose? Where does the answer lie? Let us stop, pause, and think. Man will choose life and good. **It is God's direction and man's hope that the world go forward.**

Economics, as we note in the next chapter of this book, is the main conflict between mortals. Next in importance is religion. Can the United Nations prevent the use of nuclear power? Is

there something greater than the United Nations that can prevent
the use of destructive nuclear power? Is there something more
than the United Nations requires so that man can and will make
the right choice? If there is something additional required, what
is it—and why? The proposed answer is the hope of this book
and the prayer of the author.

The answer to the interesting question above stated is found
in the achievement of UNITY OF RELIGIONS WITHIN DI-
VERSITY. You may call it vision, foresight, analytical calculation,
basic deduction, prophecy, insight, divine inspiration, cause or
effect in making a good decision or any other word or words
one may use to describe this conclusion. To the writer it is based
on spiritual research as to what constitutes Divine Law. Imagination is the eye of the spiritual world.

At the outset, we can safely state for the record that the
United Nations, by itself, can not insure peace. Man is first, last
and always a spiritual being. Without Unity of Religions within
diversity, the United Nations may fall. At the present time it is
already cracking on the surface. In time the breech may widen
and can cause it to disintegrate. Let us do everything in our
power to prevent this occurrence. The building needs shoring
and a stronger foundation. We are fighting against time, but by
the Grace of God, we are on our Father's side and events are
clearly pointing to Unity of Religions within Diversity. *The U.N.
needs as an inseparable companion—Unity of Religions within
Diversity, then the world may be safe and sound.*

Will such unity be difficult? Obviously the answer is yes.
Will it occur? The answer is definitely and enthusiastically **YES.**
In reference to a question by a Catholic Priest, as to what way
can the Jews aid in the present ecumenical movement to achieve
Christian Unity, the very learned rabbi stated: "Father, we shall
help in all ways we can and will truly pray for Christian Unity,
for when Christian Unity is achieved the lessons learned by the
Catholics and others in Christian unification will assist our two
religions in getting together." No truer words were ever spoken

by any man. Unity of Religions within Diversity is so vital that therein lies the hope, the inspiration, the longing and the prayer of mankind. Unity through the recognition of the Fatherhood of God can only come through Unity of Religions within Diversity. **THE UNITED NATIONS WILL NEVER BE ABLE TO DIRECT THE WAY OF PEACE AND LOVE WITHOUT THE UNITY OF RELIGIONS.**

We must preach and teach the truth throughout the world. We must achieve and have the correct attitude toward each other if we are to make the proper choice between life and death, between good and evil. Let us channel our thoughts with steadfast faith toward the achievement of this unity, so that so much accumulated hate and prejudice that mankind has been heir to, because of the selfishness and the ignorance of those who came before us, can be eliminated. Let us always remember the words of Jesus of Nazareth "Forgive them Father for they know not what they do." We should maintain such an attitude for it is truth and let us, by proper and dedicated education, show our opponents clearly, when we believe they are mistaken, the consequences of their erroneous thinking and the harvest of weeds that have been abundantly grown because of the errors of the past.

Wars will never be the answer to any of man's problems nor will the victor be the true judge of what is justice. Faith is the answer to all problems.

Man grips the hand of God in an unbreakable embrace when he lives with truth. LOVE CAN ONLY EXIST IN CONJUNCTION WITH THE EXERCISE OF TRUTH. For a man to say he has faith and love, and does not have truth is to make him a prize hypocrite. Without truth the entire structure of brotherhood, character, progress, unity and all of the virtues go crumbling into dust, vacant shrines. When any organization, society or nation does not have the rock of truth as its foundation, it will pass into oblivion on the stage of life. Truth is the one place where all men can meet and clasp hands in brotherly affection and love.

The so called atheist will always seek truth. *Unknowingly he seeks* God. He at times respects and uses the truth. One of the great characteristics of truth is that it is always self demonstrative. *Truth will always be the best answer that can be given in one word as to who is God.* Let us therefore teach the truth. Let us teach the truth, that THE TRUTH is God. Let us bring into reality the brotherhood of man under the Fatherhood of God by the Unity within Diversity of all of the monotheistic religions.

Man's eternal quest for Our Father will always be through the road of truth. It is the one passage that leads directly to the throne of Our Heavenly Father.

In our quest for truth let us remember that the most important statement to say of another is not that a man or woman is a GOOD CATHOLIC, A GOOD JEW, A GOOD MOSLEM, A GOOD HINDUIST, A GOOD BUDDHIST, ETC., A GOOD AMERICAN, A GOOD FRENCHMAN, A GOOD JAPANESE, A GOOD RUSSIAN, A GOOD ITALIAN, etc. NO, none of these. The truth is that the important statement is, "that a person is a GOOD MAN, A GOOD WOMAN," first last and always. To be a good person is to be in truth a good child of God and thus we are all good sons and daughters of our FATHER. Then the kingdom that Jesus and many others have died for, will become the kingdom on this earth.

In our reverence for the truth let us never deviate from a basic truth.

"IF IT IS THE TRUTH WHAT DOES IT MATTER WHO SAYS IT." Anonymous

CHAPTER II

The Causes of Human Conflicts

The main causes of conflicts among human beings arise from a love for power, selfishness, injustice, and incontinence.

Man has an inbuilt mechanism relative to the interpretation of right and wrong which makes him rebel against any injustice of his fellow man. This mechanism is called a good conscience Most individuals possess a good conscience. A good conscience is the product of good training, environment and education.

Incontinence is the failure to restrain human passions or appetites. It denotes a lack of discipline, a failure of self-mastery, which frailties may be either a product of our own irresponsibility or a result of an adverse environment or both. Arising out of such injustice, incontinence and selfishness, we then have the resultant exploitation of man by man, with its attendant avarice, pride, prejudice and hate. The use of FEAR and terror then becomes the weapon of the unjust. Freedom from such unreasonable fear is everyone's birthright. In human society, there are five fields in which conflicts arise. In their order of importance these spheres are (1) Economics (2) Religion (3) Nationalism (4) Racism and (5) Languages. The various languages are actually barriers to understanding and only in this respect are they to be regarded as constituting a cause of conflict.

ECONOMICS

Economics is the prime field in which conflicts arise. It is the continuous struggle of the haves against the have nots. Money being a medium of exchange and the means whereby material and basic needs of life are obtained, it becomes the number one goal of human endeavor. The adage, "when it comes to money, every one has the same religion," has a great deal of truth. It is a question of survival. The first law of nature is the survival of the species. This prime and strong characteristic of the human race takes precedence above all others. It was so designed by our Creator. When the attitude towards money becomes perverted, it becomes a destructive source of pride, power, domination and exploitation. *Its misuse is due to the failure to know the truth about money, and the failure of man to know his responsibility to others.*

Basically we are all spiritual beings governed by spiritual law (Divine Law) living in a spiritual world where we have all one common ancestor—GOD. The natural world is only a small part of the spiritual world. It is in the failure of man to realize this truth that causes him to make money and power the stopping place or final end of his life. Fundamentals must be taught in order that we may have wisdom and understanding.

There are four steps to man's ascendancy to the highest possible achievement in life. They are

(1) **Sensuous goals or desires.** Sensuous pleasures are the one which appeal to the senses. They are carnal pleasures, as against intellectual pleasures. A follower of sensual pleasures is known as a sensualist. There is nothing wrong in a healthy satisfaction of sensual pleasures if there is a sense of moderation, responsibility and discipline and they are channeled in divine directions. The infant gives vent to the appeasement of these innate sensual characteristics in order to survive and to learn the world around him. However, where one's complete and total goal in life is the seeking of sensual pleasures, and he makes it the sole and only end in life, they become a destructive force in his life and harmful to others. These forces must be used in a responsible manner if man is to be in control of himself. Where he is prey to these

desires, the person has failed to reach any semblance of spiritual maturity. Emotionally he is an infant.

(2) **Seeking power, glory, prestige, fame, wealth.** These desires are normal in man's ascendency. However when one makes them the sole and only end in life, disaster must follow. The complete channelling of one's talent for the feeling of power is the source of great danger to all concerned. THE LOVE OF POWER IS THE MOST DESTRUCTIVE OF ALL INTOXICANTS. The person not only degrades himself but his attitude to his fellow man is a very unhealthy one. The power mad person looks upon others as mere pawns in his pursuit for power. He does not realize wherein lies the source of all power. He operates as if he were God. The classical examples of men who believed in power as an end were men like Hitler, Mussolini, Stalin and many dictators who think that they have all the answers. Men of such calibre must be stopped not only for their own sake but also for the sake of many lives that they ill affect.

(3) **Seeking of wisdom.** This is a good step and a very good goal. When a person has attained a great love of the cultural things in life, such as the arts, poetry, music, intellectual learning, etc., he has reached a noble step upwards. Wisdom gives a person humility, dedication, love and a great appreciation of the finer and more beautiful things in life. The enjoyment of a great painting, of a beautiful opera, a fine book, the natural wonders of the universe, is the attainment of a worthy place in life. The wise person maintains an open mind.

(4) **The love of and dedication to God.** No greater achievement can be made by man, no greater height can one achieve than to wholeheartedly KNOW, LOVE AND SERVE GOD. *To serve God is to serve and help man.* The individual's work then becomes creative, humble, dedicated, loving and he becomes a benign person. His light begins to shine among men. He is a very happy person. He knows why he is here and what he should do. The intellectual fool is a person who is devoid of spiritual knowledge.

He is suffering from real poverty, spiritual poverty. No man is truly free unless and until he serves God.

The first two steps are stepping stones and not stopping places. The third and fourth step are stopping places. The best of course is always the fourth step.

Many people do not know that the top step exists. In giving a person a spiritual education one should be taught the A, B, C's of God. How can one know about God if he is not taught the attributes of God? Many errors are committed by leaders who through ignorance, do not know and teach His attributes. When we know God's attributes we know the proper road to follow. We then try to follow His laws, not from pure obedience but through understanding. They are there because He loves us and tries to show us the path to happiness. It is for this reason, that when we violate His laws we bring upon ourselves their own retribution and effect. *Through ignorance we punish ourselves.*

The spiritually mature person uses the acquisition of wealth for the unselfish betterment of the human race. Wealth then becomes a great blessing. He does not hoard his love or his wealth. LOVE'S REWARD IS LOVE. The more love we reflect the more we receive from the fountain-head of all love, God. All of the great blessings of the Almighty can be used either for good or evil. Those that have wealth have the responsibility of using their wealth in such a manner that it will help others to become self sufficient and wholesome. It should be used to build character—for which there is no substitute. Money should not be used to make a man dependent on the giver. *Money is always a tool and never an end.* It is a means by which various goals can be achieved. It should be used as a ladder and never as a crutch. Therefore, those that have achieved economic abundance have a solemn duty to help others, not by giving with one hand and taking with two, but to give wisely and wholeheartedly in order to raise the level of their fellowmen, spiritually, mentally and physically.

In the struggle between the haves and the have nots, man has disregarded the Divine Law of Equality. Equality, as the pessimists state is found in the cemetery. This is error—equality is a two way street. *Man is always striving for equality.* Let us examine this law so that we may note how it operates.

Anatomically man is the same, each person has the same nervous, auditory, ambulatory, circulatory, muscular, skeletal, visual, etc., systems. We are all co-travelers in the natural world, each with his entrance and exit. All men require minimum needs to insure a fair trip. Man will forever wage the battle for economic equality. God gives us the sun, the moon, the hills, the valleys, and the myriad beauties of nature to enjoy. The music of the birds and the wonders of nature abound in the universe. He makes no preference to any one individual. Of course we have the handicapped who have been deprived of one or more of the senses and who need our aid and understanding on the earthly trip. Fortunately we have many dedicated persons who give their love, time, money and energy to help our handicapped brothers. Many a handicapped person, through such dedication of our "miracle workers" have made their handicaps great blessings instead of liabilities.

Women are entitled to equality as teammates and are co-creators with the male sex. When the word "Man" is used it is meant also to include woman. The use of the term man expresses humanity. Woman in full maturity is the expression of love, compassion, understanding, the "Miracle worker" by whose love a person is healed more than by all the medicines in the world. She gives that ingredient in life that shows the divine brilliant spark in the human race. *Woman should always be the heart of the house.* She is the heart beat of the world when she lives the role that the Creator so richly endowed her with. When women lose their feminine qualities the human race is in dire straights. Are we facing this disaster today? Is she now seeking to be the head instead of the heart of the house? Without woman as the heart of the house, marriage and home is void of love. Is not the "heart" of vital necessity? Matriarchy can only lead a nation to ruin. *Its men will be weak.*

The striving for equality not only extends to the economic field but also to the political, social and cultural life. *What some men forget to note about the law of equality is that there is also the equality in giving as well as receiving.* These are the two sides of the coin. When we have only the taking, one is correctly designated as a parasite and the law of equality operates against him. *It is in giving that we truly receive.* It is far more blessed to give.

Where man has received certain gifts or talents from his Creator they are given to him in trust. No one picks his own talents. It is the duty of the individual to develop these talents. One must be given credit and recognition for the development of his talents. One is also to be given proper incentive rewards. The talented person should not be exploited or regimented. *However, the gifted person has the duty to use these talents unselfishly, lest they become a perversion and an evil to himself and others.* When one uses his talents for the benefit of mankind, he is a very happy person. A person is happy when he is creative and spreads happiness. It is living in accord with divine law.

Where a person may receive, let us say one talent, is he to believe that he has been cheated? The answer on critical analysis is no. The person with one talent may be able to do more for humanity than the one who has received multi-talents. There is great concentration of a gift when it is one. *God never gives sparingly but always in abundance.*

We can note the Divine Law of equality with children. The experiments are interesting. Show preference among children and note the instinctive reactions. Equality is always pleasant, inequality is always distasteful. All things being equal, equality should be given. Unequals should not be treated equally. It is not just. We would not expect the crippled or the handicapped to perform the same labor as the strong. Equality should

take into consideration the existing inequalities present in all recipients. In such cases proper allowance must be made in favor
of the handicapped.

A good illustration or metaphor of the law of equality is the
homogenization of milk. Before the discovery of homogenization,
cream came to the top of the bottle of milk. When the cream
was consumed by the selfish member of the family unit, skim
milk was left. Today we have milk which is better and every one
is satisfied. There is no preference to the aggressive one who gets
first to the icebox. Thus where money is concentrated in the
"elite" we have what is called a "financial hierarchy." This is an
evil. It is not a healthy commentary to note that in our own
country we have reached a stage where only millionaires can
compete for the presidency. Today, before an individual can
aspire to the lofty position of "President of the United States" he
must become first a millionaire. *Money has become symbolic
in the minds of the multitude as the badge of success, intelligence,
ability and the right to leadership.* It therefore confines political
strength among the wealthy. Decisions having world wide implications are then based on economic reasons to a greater extent
than warranted. The perverted all importance of wealth rubs
into the personality of the individual. We then have the worship
of a false God-idolatry. We *are* worshiping the "golden calf."
Material possessions are then used for the performance of injustices. It is one of the reasons that justice, as is later set forth, is
the number one project of the Spiritual Research Council. Materialism and theism are incompatible. Like truth and falsehood
they are diametrically opposites.

It is in the quest of materialism, that man exhibits his greatest inhumanity. *The love of money is the destruction of all that
is noble in human nature.* It is the stopping of the individual on
the second plateau of spiritual development and thus becomes a
great source of evil. It not only ruins the individual who possesses
such a perverted attitude towards money but also does untold
harm to others. In such an event hypocrisy with all of its tentacles

is seen in full extension and development. It puts to shame the only true hypocrite—the actor. Honey appears to flow from his lips, his false eloquent sincerity is spread out like the web of the spider to entrap the unsophisticated. It is all as the result of spiritual poverty. A sense of insecurity is always present.

RELIGION

Religion has and will always be a very important part in the life of man. The knowledge that there is a creator is to a great extent instinctive. Man knows that there is a power far above him, incomprehensible in scope but nevertheless ever-existing.

Great religions have grown up among men and heretofore distance and lack of communication created tremendous separations. It appears that the great separations among religions are not due to a variance of basic truths, but solely as a result of spiritual egoism.

Spiritual egoism is pride, vanity, self will and is a distinct separation from God. It is an attempt to be the equal of God, rather than the inlet and the outlet of all that there is in God. The finite can never be the infinite. When we say it is our way or no way, our truth and not your truth, it is an attempt to take the place of God among men. All of man's knowledge in the world is but a mere pittance compared to the knowledge of our Heavenly Father. *When we refuse to join hands with other religions, it is distinctly the result of wanting our own way, our own self will.* Separations and conflicts must occur and remain. Freedom of conscience, the right to worship God as one pleases is a God given right. IT IS IN FIGHTING FOR THE FREEDOMS THAT BELONG TO OTHERS THAT WE KEEP OURSELVES FREE.

The various monotheistic religions have been self confined in the past to a tremendous extent. They are now, as a result of improved methods of transportation and communication, emerging from their "own shells."

The Christian religion, for many years has felt that it had a complete monoply on the truth, that it is the one and only true and complete religion on the face of this earth. At one time the Christian religion controlled the whole world. It not only claimed great spiritual power but also temporal power. (secular power). Other fields of endeavor, such as political, scientific and industrial, fought their way, by great sacrifice to recognition and position in social and governing spheres. Religion was compelled to restrict its operation to the spiritual life of man. It is a very important sphere, yet the last two world wars were commenced by Christian nations. Why? *The answer is found in our failure to practice true Christianity, which is the religion of love, compassion, justice, aid to our brethren, and the dignity of man as a child of God.*

The lectures and the sermons that have been preached and written about love would fill libraries. Why then does man still resort to wars in an attempt to solve his problems? The answer appears to be found in that the young mind is indoctrinated with prejudice —hate. The only impregnable building that can be erected is by team-work among the various workers each doing his part. *When there is no unity we have chaos.* Religions should not try to become *THE* RELIGION by destroying the others. We can have teamwork within diversity. *There is no need for uniformity which is pure regimentation and dictatorship.*

What basic essentials must be taught by religions so all children may be saved from the prejudices and distortions that cripple them emotionally in later life? They are mainly based on fundamental truths, namely:

(1) MAN DEGRADES HIMSELF WHEN HE HATES ANY PERSON IN THE WORLD.

No one stoops so low as when he hates another human being. He enmeshes himself in the mire and muck of life and it destroys his humility and his capacity to think straight. His entire physical, mental and spiritual life is placed in imbalance. No matter what harm another person does to us, we should pray "Lord, let

me not stoop so low, become so debased as to hate any person."
Let us protect ourselves from exponents and doers of hate, from
the venal effects of their hate. Let us never hate. When we hate
another person, it warps our mentality, our mind is affected and
our health is impaired. We no longer become rational human beings. The damage that is done to one who harbors hate is tremendous. *There never is a more complete separation from God than
when we hate another human being.* The child should be taught
what are the venal effects of hate and how it is essential to avoid
hating anyone.

(2) NO MATTER WHAT THE CIRCUMSTANCES MAY BE, DO NOT ATTEMPT BY ANY MEANS WHATSOEVER TO CAUSE ANY INDIVIDUAL TO HATE ANOTHER.

When we poison the mind of another so that he is caused to
hate another person we cause the person to become deformed and
crippled. *There is no greater deformity than spiritual deformity.*
We create a polio of the soul, which has destructive implications
to the individual and to others. No matter what evil a person may
do, we have the capacity to defend, neutralize and destroy the
effects of the hate of others without hating the person. *It is the
ignorant and the vicious person who teaches the others to hate.*
Such a person uses hate for the achievement of some unholy goal
that he sets for himself. He is an individual who is always on
the first or second step of man's ascendency towards God. Many
individuals use hate in the quest for money, power, domination
or exploitation. Show me the person who hates or preaches hate
and you will find a bitter and unhappy person. We make a cardinal error when we hate. We do the correct thing when our attitude is one of *forgeting, forgiving and understanding.* We develop
the correct mental attitude toward the one who has harmed us
and we do not feed ourselves the poison and degradation that hate
engenders. *Forgiveness and love are team-mates.* One goes with
the other. No person can truly love who can not find in his heart
room to forget and forgive. By forgiving we gain spiritual

strength that gives us peace of mind, health and happiness. *Retaliation, or revenge is not sweet, it is the bitter weed that always grows at a furious rate.* It is in contravention to the teachings of Jesus.

(3) THE COMPLETE ACCEPTANCE OF RESPONSIBILITY FOR OUR ACTIONS.

The individual should be taught from a very early age that he can control, and is responsible for his actions. Too many excuses are made for the wrongdoer. Do we help the other person when we attempt to shield him from the restitution that he should make for his ill actions? Do we help the alcoholic or the delinquent when he is taught that he is a sick person? He more correctly needs aid and help through means of proper education so that he can achieve the correct attitude towards others and obtain the proper solution of his problems. How do we help the alcoholic, the delinquent, the so-called mental case, by the continuous use of a therapy that uses crutches instead of education and constructive help that can work wonders with them? There is no miracle drug that can help such individuals. *Permanent cures come from the teaching of proper attitudes and correct knowledge and proper encouragement.* A person must "know himself." The individual must be taught that his thoughts create his attitudes. Our thoughts are one place where we are King. If our actions are not good, look at the main source of trouble, our thoughts. We can therefore see how important it is for parents and those who are educators to see that what is taught to the young should be noble thoughts and thoughts of self-control and responsibility. We always reap what we sow. The seeds of life are our thoughts. Correct our thoughts and attitudes and direct them to the proper avenues and we find that we are healthy, creative and happy.

(4) THE CONSIDERATION AND REFLECTION OF OUR ACTION AND ITS EFFECT ON OTHERS.

Before we take any action we should consider its effects on others. Most errors are based on actions which are purely reflexive or impulsive. *There is action before proper digestion.* It

is tantamount to the individual eating at a fast rate of speed and
getting a stomach ache, or many of the other evils as a result of
fast eating. God is patient. Let us emulate Him in our actions.
Our actions should have reflection, rationalization, meditation, and
at times we should not hesitate to seek counsel. There is wisdom
in rational thinking. When we act in a reflexive impulsive manner, there is little or no premeditated thought used in the process.
We thus make many mistakes. At times we may face an emer-
gency and we must think fast. How often do emergencies occur?
In such a case we do the best we can and leave the rest to God.
In many cases we find that the effect of our actions on others is
not considered. Many individuals are impressionable, depending
on their ages and our relationship to them. Before major moves
are made, one should ponder well the effects of his actions on
others. *Jesus became the great teacher not so much by his teaching as by his examples.* His examples fortified the beauty of his
teaching and sincerity. Parents should always consider what the
effects of their actions are on their children. In the developing
of this positive attitude we create the unselfish viewpoint.

(5) RESPECT FOR THE OPINIONS OF OTHERS, ESPE-CIALLY WHEN THEY ARE DIAMETRICALLY OPPOSED TO OURS.

We should always listen attentively to those who hold contrary opinions to our own. *An open mind is a great blessing.*
When we close our minds, we are decaying. Like a stream that
fails to have an inlet and an outlet, our minds become stagnant.
When we feel that we have the whole truth, then we are taking
the place of God. Is there any greater error?

Many a person has been condemned as uttering a falsehood in
years gone by and later it was learned that he spoke the truth.
We should always be sensible enough TO LISTEN and to meditate
on the possible truth of the other person's statement. The failure
to keep an open mind has often been said to be "the unforgivable
sin."

(6) THE IMPORTANCE OF SELF-MASTERY IS IN THE FOLLOWING EXPRESSION.

> "Prove that you can control yourself and you are an educated man; without this, all other education is good for nothing."—Anonymous

Have religions violated these pillars of truth? Some religions advise their followers to refrain from going in other churches to hear sermons or partake in their services. Since when is practical comparative theology harmful? Why is this done? Is it a result of fear of losing a member? Does any religion preach to its followers to lie, steal, kill, etc.? Do they not all teach the golden rule? Do they not all teach love? Then why not teach by example? Why not practice the golden rule and love others as Jesus intended that we all should love.

New truths will always be discovered by man in reference to divine law. There is more about divine law that we do not know than we do know. When man reaches a direct break through from the natural world into the spiritual world, it can be stated that he has made miraculous progress. It can be done and in due time it will occur. *Religions must forget their differences,* must join hands with one another. Religion must become the greatest force of unification rather than a prime cause of division. The Party of God is under attack and humanity's hope is for Unity of Religions within Diversity.

Evangelism has become a source of rivalry for converts among some of the monotheistic religions. It is the result of fear —fear of survival and also the desire for domination. It reminds one of an occurrence which happened at a rceent Evangelical meeting where thousands were present. The Evangelist at the end of the sermon stated to his audience "Let all converts come forth and be counted." Many of the audience came to the speaker's podium. One of the converts who came up stated to the minister "I am ready to do anything that the Lord wants me to do provided however it is honorable."

Reasonable rivalry and competition is necessary, desirable and very beneficial. It stimulates progress. Without *proper* competition we would have lethargy and decadence. It sparks the onward progress of man. However, when it becomes ruthless it is tantamount to uncontrolled fire. Instead of heating and being useful it becomes a great and tremendous source of destruction. Is this the purpose of religion? Should not religion be more concerned in knowing and preaching truth and love, two great attributes of the all loving God?

Man is an intelligent animal endowed with good reason. Man is God's ideal and His workmanship is beautiful. *He endowed man with a freedom of choice, and with intelligence to make the right choice.*

When any one religion wants to be the only true religion we have spiritual egoism. To be the exclusive religion is to be monopolistic and eventually is bound to lead to chaos. *Unity of the spirit does not have room for avoidance at the dinner table nor at the wedding altar.* Why should some religions forbid (as if it were a crime) any of its members to marry someone of another religion? Why should one be prohibited from full association with another individual based alone on differences of religion? Freedom of choice, granted to man by God, should not be curtailed in any way. All men have the right to worship God as they please.

NATIONALISM

Pride in one's own country to an overexaggerated or fanatically zealous point is one of the causes for conflicts and wars. It is a severe form of national egoism, which is harmful to the individual and to the country that he belongs to. It is chauvinism, so named after Nicholas Chauvin, a soldier of Napoleon I, who in 1815, acquired much notoriety by his bellicose attachment to the lost imperial cause. It is further defined by Webster's dictionary as follows:

Absurd, unreasoning, and belligerent patriotism; the quality of being widely extravagent, demonstrative, or fanatical in regard to national glory and honor.

It is a form of extremism, as a result of a puffed ego. Present day classical examples are found in certain countries where the leaders desire to make their country the center of the universe. They are men who are not content for a place in the sun, but they desire the entire sun. There is plenty of room for each nation if it seeks cooperation with the others. There are plenty of hands ready to help.

The United Nations, although laboring, by the Grace of God is trying to do a wonderful task, in attempting to settle conflicts between nations by peaceful means. Its various activities are all in the service of peace and in the betterment of all people everywhere. It shows great prospects of creating a better world by a more efficient and harmonious relationship between nations. It needs the prayers and the sincere assistance of religion and all mankind. There is greater unity among nations today than there is among religions.

Whether the United Nations will survive is dependent upon the attitude of every individual on earth. It does appear very likely that the United Nations will be able to stand the economic storms, the distrust, the mutual existing fears, the rivalry for power, etc., with the aid of religion. *The United Nations needs* among other essentials, *Unity of Religions within Diversity*. With such Unity. the future of the United Nations as a great instrument of Peace is insured. *It cannot survive devoid of the spiritual help that religious unity within diversity will bring.* UNLESS WE ADMIT THAT GOD RULES THIS EARTH WE SHALL BE GOVERNED BY TYRANTS.

RACISM

Man foolishly has pitted himself against another based on the color of the skin. We make this serious error of judging others by our senses instead of our minds. *Sight is insight. Believing is seeing.*

Racism is an error in our attitude towards others of different races. Again in making this error of racial supremacy we have a false feeling of superiority based on visual eyesight alone. Our senses often mislead us as we depend on appearances to guide us. Underlying this alleged superiority is the concurrent exploitation, economic or otherwise of others and a violation of the additions to the Ten Commandments. The person with color should not, likewise, take advantage or exploit others because of the color he possesses. LET US ALWAYS REMEMBER THAT THE ONLY TRUE DIVISION AMONG MEN, FROM NOW THROUGHOUT ALL OF ETERNITY, WILL BE CHARACTER. Any other division is non-existent. *We are all children of the same Father.*

LANGUAGE

The language conflict is in actuality a barrier or a negative quantity. It impedes people from really knowing each other. It is not difficult for everyone to learn at least two languages, his native tongue and also a universal language. Pride, the greatest fault of man, will delay man in the acceptance of a universal language or method of communication. Fortunately, knowledge of the English language is spreading a great deal throughout the world. However, we should teach another language to all children in elementary school, when they are capable of easily absorbing another language. It should be one of their own choosing. Many subjects are taught, that pupils do not use or need and shortly forget and discard. Knowing another language is always a great asset.

CHAPTER III

The Effect of the Triune Doctrine

Certain beliefs by certain sects of Christianity give rise to conflicts, the real causes of which are trivial and of little or no significance. One of these conflicts is the Trinity, also known as the Triune doctrine. God is believed to be three persons, one is the Father, the second is the Son and the Third is the Holy Ghost. It is the division of the Almighty in three distinct units which are alleged to be part of the whole. The Triune Doctrine is not explained by all Christian religions under the same basis. Under such a doctrine, the Father is referred to as God, the Father of all things and all persons, the Son is referred to as Jesus Christ, true God and true man and the third is referred to as the Holy Ghost, which is the heavenly spirit, through which God pours his beneficence to man.

The Trinity in man refers to the physical, spiritual and mental life of man. The body is the physical expression, the mind embraces the mental life and the spiritual life embodies the soul (The Christ) and the immortal life or part of man. This is not to be confused with the Triune doctrine. The explanation of the Trinity is very often confusing not only to the parishioners but also to the exponents or teachers of the doctrine.

Cardinal Cushing sums up the difficulty in a very trite story that he often tells. He states

"A pedestrian was struck by an automobile and seriously injured. A catholic priest happened to be passing by and rushed over to give him aid. While awaiting the arrival of the ambulance, the priest decided to give the injured person the last rites. He bent over the dying man and asked "Do you believe in God the Father, God the Son, and God the Holy Ghost?" The dying man opened his eyes and responded, "Father, I am dying and you are asking me riddles."

The Trinity referred to in this story is somewhat different than the trinity referred to in reference to the aspects of man's nature. We shall scrutinize the origin of the Three persons constituting the Godhead of the diety, the purpose for the enunciation of this doctrine, the conflicts that have arisen and why it is a block towards Unity of Religions within Diversity. We shall take up the proper attitude toward the Trinity, its relative importance to religious belief and its significance and importance as a spiritual doctrine.

How did the Trinity originate? As christianity progressed various conflicts and differences arose. The biggest dispute was over the nature of Jesus. A priest named Arius maintained that Jesus being a human being, was created by God and naturally because of his finite nature could not be the equal of God. This was known as Arianism. Another priest, Athanasius, selected by Bishop Alexander, opposed this view and insisted that Jesus was the equal of God. In order to secure a certain uniformity, Constantine, the ruler of the Roman Empire, called an assembly or council of bishops. This council met in 325 A.D. at the town of Nicea in Asia Minor, not far from Constantinople. About three hundred bishops or their representatives attended this meeting, and it was the first council of the Roman Catholic Church. The two factions expounded their respective views and then the matter was put to a vote. The council accepted the logic or reasoning of Athanasius and condemned Arius as a heretic. Thus was formulated the Nicene Creed. A short resume of the situation is related by the Unitarian Universalist in a booklet written by John Nicholas Booth, wherein he states:

"How did the idea that Jesus was God gain wide acceptance? One of the church fathers named Athanasius persuaded a council of disputing bishops at Nicea, in 325, to accept a creed for the entire church which would henceforth specify that Jesus' nature was the same as God's. Millions of Christians have accepted this decision of a small band of early religious leaders, meeting in Asia Minor, *who were less well informed than the majority of modern clergymen.* Unitarian Universalists believe that the creedal doctrine of the Trinity is neither factual nor significant in religion." (Page 13)

Are we fair to Jesus when we pronounce and set forth the doctrine of the Trinity? Do we in truth do justice to this great man? Do we cause people not to follow Christianity because of the Trinity doctrine? *IS IT THE TRUTH?* Is it really a unifying force?

In the determination of these questions we must again re-member that only in knowing the truth will man be free. It is seeking and knowing the truth that we will find God. *If we truly and sincerely love God we must love the truth.* One of the essen-tial elements of truth is that truth cannot be made truth simply by human pronouncements or legislative fiat. *Truth is only truth when it is part of Divine Law.* Man can never know Divine law with positiveness. Man however, in his study of divine law. because of its unchangeable qualities and orderly occurence can in many cases state that a particular occurence is divine law, be-cause it is part of unfailing divine order.

A well known theologian, Dr. James A. Pike, stated in a sermon on August 30, 1964 that the Trinity is not necessary. He is a Protestant Episcopal Bishop of California, and previous to his ministry was a Catholic and a lawyer. He is sincere. He stated:

"The doctrine that distinguishes the Father, the Son and the Holy Ghost as components of the diety was not among the original teachings of Christianity. Our Lord never heard of it. The apostles knew nothing of it. The doctrine of the Holy Ghost is due to the influence of Greek thought on early Christian philosophers. Such

a doctrine causes confusion or an undesirable tendency to tri-
theism (a belief in three Gods—a polytheism). All of the
qualities that are attributed to the Holy Spirit can be said of God
himself without distinguishing a third person. God has been
creating all along, we don't need a shop steward. God has always
been redeeming. Read the old Testament. The tenets of orthodox
Christian faith can be retained while eliminating the separateness
of the Holy Spirit altogether. The doctrine of the Trinity is
something that man made up. The concept of the Trinity is a
piece of very heavy luggage on the backs of our missionaries
around the world. Jesus warned us against putting new wine in
old vessels lest the vessels break. Why should we impose on new
converts something which the apostles would not have understood themselves."

This sermon was given by Bishop Pike as a guest speaker at
the Church on Broadway and Wall Street, in Manhattan, New
York City.

The deity theory, upon which the Trinity is based will always be a block to religious unity. It is not necessary and
impedes the blending of the Unity of the monotheistic religions
within diversity. **RELIGIONS THAT PROFESS THAT JESUS
IS GOD ARE NEITHER FAIR AND JUST TO JESUS NOR ARE
THEY JUST TO OTHERS.** Let us love Jesus for the great gift
he really is, for the tremendous wealth of Divine Law he has
furnished us. *Let us thank God that a man like Jesus was born
and lived among mankind.* Let us use his great wisdom to really
build the edifice of Unity of Religions within Diversity. Let us
spread true Christianity and not change Jesus so that he would
not recognize himself. In attempting to make Jesus God, we violate one of the Ten Commandments. *Jesus never said he was God.*
Any interpretation or statement that he did say he was God is
false. We have and shall always impede true spiritual growth as
long as we maintain such a falsehood. *We can preach an untruth
one million years and we shall gain nothing but heartaches.* The
harm that such a falsehood creates will far outweigh any good.

To know God we must know the truth, only then will man be free. As long as we teach the young, whose custody rests in our care, with falsehoods, we shall reap the twisted minds, the hatreds, and prejudices and the conflicts among men. Let us love the truth. Let us build the house Jesus has started on the true rock and honest foundation that it rightfully deserves. How can we ever have Unity of Religions within Diversity when we insist upon teaching the deity theory and makes a mortal human being God? Did not Jesus say that the kingdom of God is within all of us, that His Father and Our Father is one?

The deification of an individual is as old as mankind. In religion, where we have a genius who by his teaching uplifts mankind, we find that his followers elevate him to the position of God. In order to further this teaching we impregnate his birth with the idea of a virgin birth. We have him conceived without the necessity of the male parent. We take all of God's law and suspend its action and make the individual God himself. The words of Shakespeare are well noted "Oh, what a web we weave when we first start to deceive." We start with one falsehood and then compound the crime with others. *Our foundation must become weak and our good works are diminished. In using such a method we are very unjust to the person we deify.* We can preach the untruth for ages, in time such untruth must be acknowledged if we are to climb higher in our ascent upwards and to be strong spiritual beings. In seeking the truth man will always advance closer and closer to God. He cannot ascend upwards as long as he teaches untruths. A religion grows when it omits from its teachings any untruth. *When we fastened our hopes, our expectations, our will and our love to truth, we indeed fastened our life to the service of God.* We must not be afraid to change and to admit our errors. It is human to err.

The acceptance of untruths for the purpose of obtaining a certain advantage is being shortsighted. Our present gain will always be a shackle to weigh us down in the future. Only the truth continuously goes forward. We should not use untruths for the purpose of compromising. It is the wrong instrument to use. There can never be any compromise with the truth. *To compromise with the truth is saying that in this particular case we do not need God. God can never be eliminated.* His laws are unfailing and they never have an exception. If divine order were to fail for one second the world would collapse. Man must, because of his imperfection, always make allowances for his mistakes. God, because he is perfect, need not make any exceptions. Perfection is perfection because of its complete unfailing accuracy. Can the correct answer to a problem in arithmetic be changed or compromised? Can any of God's laws ever fail to work or to operate?

What is the main reason for the Trinity? What is the purpose of such a doctrine?

The main reason for the preaching of the Trinity appears to be that dormant scoundrel in man—a quest for power. Is it not egotistical to teach your followers that God in truth founded your church, that God himself came on this earth as man and endowed us with His vision and infallibility? Is it not self-deceit to believe that your religious organization is the only mouthpiece of God? Do we do the right thing when we have our fellow human beings pay homage by prayer to a deceased person as an intermediary before God? *Does God need an ambassador?* Do we need a lawyer at the bar of Divine justice? Does not God love us with an everlasting devotion. Can we not always turn to him for help, guidance and wisdom? Is not God always and at all places ready to listen to all of His children? Have we not all received one insurance policy because of our human birth and that is His unfailing and eternal love? Can we ask for more? Then why should we place untruths before people and thus cause many persons to turn away from God or become so called atheists?

One great block to Unity of Religions within diversity is Biblical theology, where the Bible is accepted in its entirety as the complete word and truth in all details. We must all concede that the Holy Bible is one of the greatest books ever written by man. However, we again do not do justice to the inspired authors of the Bible when we attempt to convey the theory that every word in the Bible is the truth, and that in each and every respect it is the word of God.   If we were to follow the Bible in all respects we would institute capital punishment for trivial infractions, which today are not even classified as minor crimes.   The Bible should be studied as a history of the spiritual evolvement of man upwards to his creator, and for its great depth of divine law which it teaches and expounds.

The virgin birth, the resurrection and the assumption are all beliefs which should not be forced on others. *Let us teach the religion of Jesus rather than the religion about Jesus.* Can we find more beautiful and greater wisdom than found in the New Testament?   Can any one doubt the genius of St. Paul and mankind's great debt to him?

The religion about Jesus is the cause of much confusion, conflicts and errors. *It is the duty of religion to preach the truth, the whole truth and nothing but the truth.* We should not preach any doctrine which is not true just because it might sound beautiful if it were the truth. *We cannot trifle with God. We can not preach the truth about God except by the use of the truth.* When we preach untruths we cause many clear thinking individuals to stay away from all religions.   People cannot be guided by the use of opiates.   One must get to the cause of the disturbance.   To use untruths is to dull minds into insensibilities and errors.

Let us love and pay homage to Jesus by the use of truth.

GREATER IS THE MAN WHO ADMITS HIS MISTAKES THAN THE ONE WHO COVERS OR EXCUSES THEM, FOR IN THE FIRST THERE IS AN OPPORTUNITY FOR CORRECTION, WHILE IN THE LATTER THERE IS ONLY THE ELEMENT OF CONTINUANCE.

CHAPTER IV

Aspects of Unity

The great problem which all of the major religions must shortly face is the necessity of unity within diversity. *It has reached the stage where there is no choice.* **It is either unity or destruction.** *It is love or perish.*

What do we mean by Unity. Unity is harmony, cooperation, joy, sharing, love, God, order, progress, life and peace. This definition is not meant and is not to be understood to be complete or absolute, which divine attribute belongs to God alone. **To define is to confine.**

The present need for religious unity within diversity is one of critical importance. Rev. Eric Butterworth of the Unity School of Christianity very aptly explained the situation in the following words: "The great need in the world today is unity. Only through unity can we find the cooperation and spontaneous sharing that must bridge the gaps between warring factions of men, as individuals, in groups, or as nations. And only through unity can the individual who has fallen victim to the warlike conflicts of his own mind find a sense of integration of spirit, soul, and body— only through unity can he find inner peace, and poise and power. Yes, the world needs unity . . . among nations, *within and among religions*, between labor and management, *in the unreal divisions of humankind made real by prejudices.*"

One of the greatest research spiritual scientist of our times, Dr. Marcus Bach, author of "Make It an Adventure," published by Prentice-Hall, Englewood Cliffs, N.J., and numerous other books,

stressed the need for unity and the attributes required of religions
in order to achieve this goal. He stated:

"A new world order must have a spiritual basis and that this
must be more than a mere phrase or a narrow sectarian approach.
It must be built upon unity in diversity, a recognition of our com-
mon heritage as children of God, and most of all, upon an act of
faith."

In order to understand the need for unity, we must first understand our relation to God and to each other.

All men possess a oneness with the life, substance and intelligence of God. ALL MEN ARE BROTHERS. *Unity within di-*
versity is the yearning of all of humanity. This yearning, in order
to achieve a greater degree of peace, must be filled.

"Have we not all one father? Hath not one God created us?
Why then doth every one of us despise his brother, violat-
ing the covenant of our fathers?"
                                        Malachias 2,10

At times religions, because of their separations, make this
fundamental and basic truth of brotherhood very difficult for the
individual to understand.

For the first time in the history of religions, organized religions face a common attack from communism, an extremely powerful foe. Before religions can envision the best way of meeting
the challenge, it is necessary to attempt, within the realms of
human capacity and ability, to see as clearly as possible the
reasons for the development of communism, especially as it pertains to and affects religion. Let us attempt to be as honest and
as just as our abilities permit, not only to ourselves but also to
our enemies.

"We ought always to deal justly, not only with those who are just to us, but likewise to those who endeavor to injure us, and this for fear lest by rendering them evil, we should fall into the same vice."

Hierocles

"He that would make his own liberty secure must guard even his enemy from oppression; for if he violates this duty, he establishes a precedent that will reach to himself. It is much safer to reconcile an enemy than to conquer him; victory may deprive him of his poison, but reconciliation of his will."

Owen Feltham

"To love an enemy is the distinguished characteristic of a religion which is not of man but of God. It could be delivered as a precept, only by him who lived and died to establish it by his example. It is the enemy whom we do not suspect who is the most dangerous."

Fernando Rojas

"Have you fifty friends? It is not enough. Have you one enemy? It is one too much."

Italian Proverb

Our enemies are entitled to justice. Why is it important to be just to your enemies? In feeding our enemy we remove fear. He does not become as tense. He becomes more secure and starts to relax. The cold war has not eased considerably. Tension is the product of fear—fear of survival, fear of a threat to one's security and freedom. When we act as a friend, we decrease the poison of poisons, fear. The attitude of our opponent must change. This of course is assuming that we have a normal person to deal with. The selling of wheat showed the Russians that we are willing to share. They realize that we are good and that their attitude towards us is greatly mistaken. We do not prevent them from learning from us how to grow wheat and other foods. We extend a friendly hand despite the fact that we have mighty muscles. Our moral intellect is even superior to our physical force. In acting in this method, we can always rest assured that we are following divine law. We do not seek to destroy our enemy but we attempt in every way possible and with a divine love of patience to make them know we are team mates and brothers *as we are in veritas.*

WE ARE GODLIKE WHEN WE ARE JUST TO OUR ENEMIES. IT BRINGS THE KINGDOM OF GOD ON THIS EARTH.

What is communism? Communism is a revolution. It is a revolution not only against the so-called capitalistic system but also against religion. It is very ruthless and aggressive.

Karl Marx, the exponent of communism, adopted certain concepts as the heart of his writing. His concept "from each according to his ability and to all according to their needs" has had tremendous impact in our time. Another concept is that "religion is the opiate of the people." Communism is therefore a two prong offensive. It has made tremendous progress in the development of nuclear energy and by brute force have subjugated the surrounding countries of Poland, Austria, Hungary, Bulgaria, Rumania and Czechoslovakia. They have drawn an iron curtain running from the Baltic Sea to the Adriatic Sea. A short time ago Cuba became a communistic stronghold. Germany and Viet Nam have been divided into two zones, namely the communistic and the democratic or western sphere. Communism is making its strongest appeal on the important problem of necessities that has always faced man. Food, shelter and clothing are some of the basic requirements of life. *Religion has no meaning or importance to a starving man. He is pre-occupied with survival.*

Let us view the reasons for the troubled waters. *Nothing happens because of divine accident.* Some say that communistic belief is pure atheism. This opinion is subject to error. The fact that one denies God, by his denial does he not admit the existence of a superior intelligence? *Does not the liar know the truth?* Have not the Russian leaders come to the conclusion that there is a divine power that exists? Have not their intricate calculations in scientific research proved to them the existence of profound order in the universe? Do not their leaders use the word "sacred" in referring to actions of men? Have they not realized that man is incurably religious? *They are not stupid by any means and we should never underestimate their ability or cunning.* They are strongly motivated and are and will always be very strong antagonists. The fight will not be an easy one. *They have patience,* are flexible and they know some of our frailties. *They have dedication.* They believe in the value of giving and have a passion for knowledge. They know the importance of an education.

What are the reasons for the revolution of communism against religion? It appears to be a distinct challenge in the following respects:

1. A refusal to believe in the God explanation given and practiced by religion.

2. Disagreement as to the truth preached by religion.

3. A fixed attitude that religion is a divisive and detrimental force rather than creative and progressive.

4. That religion is the opiate of the people.

5. That Russian communism or humanism is superior to religion as a way of life.

Russian communism is an outgrowth of Christianity. *It is a product of the west and not of the east.* This will be touched upon in latter portions of this book.

There are many questions that we can ask ourselves in an attempt to see what basis in truth has led to the communistic revolution. A few of them are—Is the explanation and definition of God given by the various religions adequate and true? What were the injustices that caused the revolution? In what way did religion fail to stand for the elimination of injustices among men? How and in what manner did religion fail to serve mankind?

Truth requires an honest self appraisal if it is to be constructive. RELIGION SHOULD HELP MAN TO FIND THE TRUTH AND TO MAKE THE HUMAN BEING KIND TO HIS BROTHERS. WE ARE IN TRUTH ALL CHILDREN OF THE SAME FATHER-GOD. WE ARE A SPIRIT OF GOD.

Have religions been open minded or have some of them closed the ends? Have they realized that one of the undeniable attributes or qualities of God is progress? Have they fought progress and truth? Have religions admitted, as do other organizations in the world, that they are fallible and incomplete? Have they acted with compassion and understanding in their dealings with their co-religionists? Have they properly fulfilled the direction and teachings of Jesus? Have they vied with one another for converts by unfair methods and criticism that spread hate instead of love? Have they helped their co-religionists as brothers should? Have they put too much emphasis and concern on materialism and on rituals? Have they preached and lived by the law of retaliation? Have they paved the way of man in the direction of love and taught their followers what is love and what to do and what to refrain from? Have their examples been outstanding? Have they taken care of their own workers or ministers in adversity, sickness and age? Have they preached one law to be used in the market place and another to be followed in their own organization? Have they shut their eyes to the misdeeds of their own members while condemning those on the outside? Have they spiritually united with their fellow theologian of other faiths, to help each other better understand and research HIS laws? Have they advocated the repeal of capital punishment (murder masquerading as justice) throughout the world? Have they embraced the Scientist as one of the greatest of all of God's workers who helps us to grow toward God? (There is far more religion in science than there is science in religion). Have they placed form in place of substance? Is there opium in religion?

The basic element of religion should be TRUTH.

Let us try to state and explain God, in simple words that everyone can understand, with the realization and remembrance of the ever present limitations of the human mind, the inadequacy of words and our mode of expression.

God is spirit. Thoughts are the vital currents of the spiritual and natural world. Thoughts are the substance of which we are composed. God is invisible, the same as electricity. No one will ever see God with his eyes nor ever see electricity. (We can however see God in man and in his wonderful work. To believe is to see. HE is substance and that part of man which is immortal. HE is all in all. HE is what we are. All of us are His children, his expression, his idea, and we, therefore, are all related to one another. HE is the creator of everything and his spirit is in all life and matter, varying only in degree. He is the one father-mother. He is the I AM. (The true teaching of God as the I Am has been neglected.)

What is the I AM? Briefly, the I AM is God's name and the name of God (His spirit) in us. When we speak of others, God's name is HE IS, SHE IS, YOU ARE, WE ARE, THEY ARE. When we speak of the universe His name is IT IS. Therefore, we should be careful to use His name in a creative and respectful manner. When we mention, think or use His name in a negative or adverse manner we harm ourselves. When we think or speak well of others and of ourselves, we give reverence to His name and thereby achieve good results. Thusly, we realize the meaning and significance of the Commandment: "Thou shalt not take the name of the Lord Thy God in vain."

We know that some of the attributes of electricity are light, heat and power. What are the attributes of God. God is everything that is good that the human mind can think of. He is everything that is positive and creative. There are no negative qualities or attributes in God. To enumerate a few, God is Joy (perfect love), truth, peace, mind, equality, progress, abundance, humor, science, harmony, health, life, optimism, patience, courage, intelligence, beauty, glory, power, order, compassion, etc. HE never returns evil for evil, hate for hate, but returns good for evil and love for hate. *He is not an avenging God.* God never does anything to give us sorrow. Man may disown God, but God never disowns man. HE is one father-mother who never abandons his children at any time or under any circumstances. *We cannot separate ourselves from Him.* To reach Him is to think about HIM. It is that simple. He has given us the universe as HIS heirs and with HIS continuous and unfailing love and intelligence *to enjoy it with others.* There is an abundance of room in HIS house and plenty of food on HIS banquet table. HIS telephone line is never busy. There is no end to the knowledge and accomplishments of man. There is only one permanent limitation. *Our knowledge will always end where HIS begins.* Did not Jesus say:

"You therefore are to be perfect, even as your Heavenly
Father is perfect."
St. Matthew 5:48

Although the extent of our knowledge is increasing at a very fast rate of speed, man will not be able to create life. Any attempt to create life is tantamount to seeking perpetual motion. *God's knowledge starts with life. Therein lies the permanent limitation of man's knowledge.*

The cry is often raised, why is there so much evil in the world? Is GOD powerless to remedy the situation? What is evil? If we knew the full explanation and could define evil in exact words we would be the wizard of wizards. No one can truly define evil. It is a relative term. What may be good or food for one person is harmful or poison to another. Some nations may enact legislation which is contrary to Divine law, and we then say that the violation of the law is criminal and thus evil. What may be unlawful in one locality may be legal in another. Sometimes the difference may be across a river or a stream. No matter what

explanation we give to evil, it appears to be ineffable. It has
many characteristics which do not lend themselves to a plausible
explanation. (See Encyclopedia of Religion by Vergilius Fern).
Evil, however, does have some definite trademarks. It is real and
not illusory. We do have a great deal of evil in the universe.
Perhaps it is a challenge by the Almighty God to bring man
closer together and to increase man's love for another. *If there
was no choice between good and evil would character ever develop?* Man can do a great deal to reduce the evil in the world.
In freedom there is responsibility. Man will reduce evil as he in-
creases his love for one another. It appears to have a direct relation and connection to love. The more love we emanate the
lesser becomes the poison or evil. *Prayers can move mountains.
Love can move the world.* Evil, therefore, is a challenge for man.
The command from God is one to eradicate evil. Many diseases
have been eliminated that at one time were the scourge of mankind. A great deal of evil stems from ignorance. Perhaps all of
evil can be laid to the door of ignorance—*ignorance of His laws.*
Evil is found in emotional immaturity, called spiritual infancy in
theology. It is in many cases the incomplete development of the
good in the individual or the failure of the individual to adjust
creatively to a particular environment. It may be the result of a
hostile environment. Does not the fig tree grow beautiful and
impervious to many diseases in a warm climate and fail to thrive
in a cold climate? *Man is always greatly affected by the particular environment or mores of the locality in which he lives.* Oft
times evil is the immature or unripened fruit. It needs nourishment (quality education), pruning, (discipline, self-mastery) and
love to bring it to full ripeness. The flower which has bloomed
and the individual who unfolds to his full potential are always
beautiful. Evil is the direct result of the separation of man from
God, due mostly to man's lack of knowledge of God and his stub-
borness in seeking his own will. The mature and noble person shows
his intelligence and spiritual depth by being dedicated, by being
kind and by his love for all humanity. **No person is truly intelligent who is not kind, who has not heart.** A real person does not

get tired of doing good. Ingratitude doesn't deter or stop his continuance to help others.

Sometimes individuals cannot understand why their prayers
are not answered. A little girl named Diana prayed for a bicycle.
Her girl friends who had bicycles knew of her daily prayers. Her
parents could not afford to give her one, as money was required
for basic needs. One of Diana's friends chided her one day and
said, "Diana, you have prayed and prayed to your God for a bicycle and He has never answered your prayers." Diana, responded
"Oh yes He has. He answered No." Many times our prayers
appear not to be answered and as spoiled children we cannot take
what we feel is a no for an answer. Is our frustration tolerance
very low?

It is indeed a blessing and we should be thankful that God
does not always give us what we want. HE knows what is good
for us and we should understand that what appears to us to be
His refusal is for our benefit and not for HIS: Divine law never
fails to operate. In actuality there is no "no" in God. God is only
a giving God.

What are religions? A very good answer is found in the definition given by Dr. Marcus Bach:

"Religions are the various dialects by which men speak to
God!"

*NO MAN IS TRULY RELIGIOUS UNLESS HE LOVES ALL
RELIGIONS.*

No one can deny the tremendously valuable work that religions have made in uplifting man to a higher plane of understanding and love of the Almighty God. *Religion is a necessity.*
It is the sum total of all that there is in life. It is a required
ingredient to bring humanity to nobility and maturity. *It is the
heartbeat of the world.* Religion gives one a sense of purpose and
religionists should teach and advise their flock in progressive

practical and creative paths. A truly spiritual person is better able to endure colossal misfortune, suffering, frustration, danger and uncertainty. He knows that there is an everpresent and dependable companion with him at all times. There never will be any government that can long endure without religion among its people. *No government can drive God from the minds of their people. HIS eternal presence and their foolishness are too obvious.*

Proof of the greatest unification, integration and cohesiveness of religion is found in the history of the Jew. Even though widely separated because of persecutions, for over two thousand years, without a homeland, they have retained their identity and have kept together. Their unity lies in their allegiance to God.

The execution by the Romans of Jesus was a pure "political fix" (the determination of a legal controversy not based on the merits) and a judicial murder. Jesus was magnanimous and understood the spiritual ignorance of his prosecutors and executioners. He asked our Heavenly Father to forgive them as they did not know what they were doing. Nevertheless, so called Christians have persecuted the Jew as "Christ Killers" (Deicides —God killers—can we kill God?) for almost two thousand years. *BY WHAT CONCEPT OF JUSTICE, MUST THE SONS BE PUNISHED FOR THE SIN OF THEIR EARTHLY FATHERS?* (Deut. 24. 16).

The injustice done to the Jew far outweighs their crime in the participation of the "political fix" of the original group of Jews who took part in the plot to persecute and condemn Jesus. The respective crimes are so out of proportion that it shocks the justice of God. LET US CORRECT, ALTHOUGH BELATED, ONE OF THE GRAVEST CRIMES PERPETRATED ON OUR BROTHER JEW. Let us never forget that our great heritage "The Holy Bible" is a Jewish-inspired book. Can we call ourselves Christians when we do not follow the example and counsel of our leader? Inharmony is always the result of injustice *Love and injustice are always incompatible.*

JESUS HAS NOT BEEN FOLLOWED. His teachings have been so warped, misconstrued and adulterated that if he were to walk this earth again, he would not recognize his followers. *To be a true Christian is very difficult.*

Have the Christian churches failed to follow Jesus? It appears that they are all guilty of this error in varying degrees. Jesus is to religion what Thomas Edison and Charles Steinmetz are to electricity and what Dr. Albert Schweitzer is to medicine. Jesus's knowledge of spiritual law was tremendous. *He was indeed a spiritual scientific genius.* Did not Jesus state in no uncertain terms:

> "Think not that I am come to destroy the law, or the prophets, I am not come to destroy but to fulfill."
>
> Matthew 5:17

> "This is my commandment, that you love one another as I have loved you. Greater love than this no one has than that one lay down his life for his friends. By this all men will know that you are my friends, if you have love for one another."
>
> John 15:12,17

Christianity had its birth in the cradle of man's inhumanity to man and has continuously been involved in gigantic struggles since its inception up to the present time, although its spiritual leader has always preached the great principle of non-resistance and peace. What a strange occurrence! Jesus tried to uproot the law of retaliation, or of exact requital (measured justice) deeply ingrained in the old testament and substitute for "An eye for an eye, a tooth for a tooth and a life for a life" *the law of Love.* I Corinthians 13.

Judaism gave us Jesus and the other Jews who by devoted zeal and courage developed Christianity. *Judaism is the parent of Christianity.* The son, Christianity, has shown his ingratitude to his parents by prejudice and wrongs that one would do well to immediately correct and forget.

We owe the Jews a great debt of gratitude. Rev. Robert W. Gleason, a leading Roman Catholic theologian and chairman of the Fordham University Department of Theology stated in a sermon given in St. Patricks Cathedral in January 1962 "No Christian can ever thank Israel sufficiently for the gift of Christ. To have entered with joy into Israel's inheritance and to fail in gratitude to her would be ignoble, base, unchristian, unfilial. And yet, Christians, historically, have been ungrateful." We are still ungrateful. (See also Christian Tradition and Anti-Semitism, by Rabbi Marc H. Tannebaum, Herald Tribune, August 10, 1964, page 15.)

The religions of the world and their various denominations are each a restriction of one's view. It is looking at God through a certain limited aperture or opening. One day a minister of one of the Christian sects, (which number about three hundred) was attempting to persuade a certain young man to be more active in his church, the religion of his fathers. The minister pointed out that it was important to be a participating member of the church, that this would give him the needed sense of belonging, of security, of power and prestige, that it was his duty to attend services regularly each week and to support his church, etc. The young man listened attentively and replied "Reverend, I believe in everything you say, but why restrict me to one dish when I like the smorgasboard? Furthermore, I earn my living from members of other churches and therefore am able to help support my own church."

Every religion is beautiful. *RELIGIONS ARE THE FLOWERS AND THE MUSICAL INSTRUMENTS OF THE SPIRITUAL WORLD.* Each religion has tremendous wisdom, love and understanding. Each religion is an uplifting influence and has a very high moral code. They are necessary institutions in any society. A Russian commissar admitted that "Religion is like a nail, the more you hit it, the deeper it penetrates into the wood." Only recently a Russian female biologist and a "convinced atheist" referring to Karl Marx's statement that "religion is the opiate of

the masses" stated, "If religion is the opiate, it should be stated
that narcotics in small doses can be useful and beneficial, can
calm people and lessen pain."

All religions have their great prophets and their sacred writings. Each believes in one God and the sanctity of human life.
Each attempts to increase the capacity of the individual to love.
Each attempts to express the same truths in different ways. All
have deep faith that the spirit of God within us all continues
after what we call death occurs. *The world would be a jungle of
beasts were it not for religions.* There is always spiritual evolu-
tion continuously unfolding itself for the advancement and the
betterment of man.

*The differences between religions are but mere trifles. Yet
they have become like granules of sand magnified to such an
extent that they appear like mountains.* Language barriers between theologians should not be a handicap. Many can speak
numerous languages. At the present time the spiritual lens is out
of focus. It needs alignment and adjustment. We need more
spiritual light in order to obtain greater wisdom.

"Where the pupil of the eye is missing there is no light;
where there is no knowledge there is no wisdom."
                                        Sirach 3,24

Let us see whether or not God has any religious denomination
or color. A good understanding of the aspects or attributes of
God can help us gain the proper perspective. Is God a Moslem,
Buddhist, Christian, Taoist, Jew, Hindu, Confucianist or any other
religious denomination? God is all inclusive. He is the creator
of color. HE IS COLOR. He is invisible spirit. A very fine
article on this subject appeared in the February 28th, 1959 issue
of the Saturday Review of Literature, written by Norman Cousins,
who also handles this question in a very interesting manner:

"Is God a Christian?" He says, "If Christians insisted on an affirmative answer to this question as a pre-condition for a unified approach to the overriding needs of our time, then they are apt to discover that the large majority of God's children don't agree with them. For the combination of man's sovereign individuality and his geographical separation have produced a glittering variety of relgious experience. Up to now, remoteness have made possible Great Separations. But a suddenly compressed world has now made mandatory a Great Confrontation—for religion and for everything else—and what is required today is not the absorption of all religions into a common theology but a common resolution to mount a common attack on a common problem in a common cause. If what we seek to do is to utilize the spiritual resources of men in meeting their problem at its largest, then these resources will have to come from Christian and Jew, from Moslem and Hindu, from Buddhist and Taoist, from Confucian and Bahai. But if the individual representatives in this grand spiritual concourse draw away the moment there is a variance from a particular theology, then the possiblity of common action is destroyed. We may not be able to persuade Hindus that Jesus and not Vishnu should be paramount on their spiritual horizon, nor Moslems that Lord Buddha is at the center of their spiritual universe, nor Hebrews that Mohammed is the major prophet, nor Christian that Shinto best expresses their spiritual concerns, to say nothing of the fact that we may not be able to get Christian to agree among themselves about their own relationships to God. But what we can do is to try at least to get all to agree to the human proposition that spiritual resources are inherent in all men, that these resources, when summoned, can bring them closer to one another, and that the sacredness of life is not peculiar to any one creed. . . . Religion need not turn against itself to do that which is now necessary. A basic unity already exists. That unity resides not in doctrine but in man himself. The existence of the human conscience is a prime element of that unity. Theology cannot survive without man. Theology therefore can transcend itself in the cause of man."

How do other faiths feel about Unity of Religions with Diversity? Let us see what the attitude of the Moslems may be.

One of the brilliant spokesman of the Moslems, Amadou Hampate Ba, who resides in Bamako, Republic of Mali, Africa, and

who is now Ambassador to the Ivory Coast Republic, in a letter
dated November 3, 1961, addressed to this writer, stated:

"We shall never be too many getting together so that the
party of God may live and so that the Spirit may conserve
its rights. It is only under this condition that the human
being can go on, in peace, to his ascension toward the
Sublime and toward True Liberty.

Every conflict, on this earth, conceals a cause that is
materialistic, scurrilous or subtle; the cause of the divisions
among human beings.

Men who live in God, whatever may be their religion,
must be interdependent (unite). **They will never know
that they are true brothers until the day when those who
deny God would have the upper hand.** That day, which
we hope we shall never see, would be, if it were to arrive,
the day when all the believers in God would be condemned
to the same slavery.

You and I have in common this principal idea which
aims to eliminate, as you say so well, this spirit of competition in matters of religion.

The great son of the Holy Virgin, our Lord Jesus Christ,
taught love of neighbor.

The messenger of God, Mohammed, instituted in Islam
the duty of greeting your neighbor by wishing him divine
peace and grace.

Before the time of these two Masters (Christ and Mohammed), Moses made his people flee in order to assure
them peace against despotism.

This leads me to say that the three great monotheisms
of the present day: Judaism, Christianity and Islamism
(Mohammedanism) are based on three principles: Love,
Charity and Peace.

When this truth has really taken possession of one, he
will be able to rise above himself. And once he has gone
beyond the boundary of self-love, a state which I shall call
"spiritual infancy," we shall sprout wings which will permit us to fly on high and soar above, contemplating the
different religions, which will appear like landscapes in the
immeasurable divine spheres.

All my life I have struggled so that religion will not be
the result of compulsion, but the result of conviction.

Mohammed, the Prophet of God, said that he preferred one man converted by conviction to a thousand men coming to Islam through fear of the sword.

If religions wish to survive the historical events which are about to overthrow the habitual order of humanity, it will be necessary that they unite (unionize). I apologize for using this popular expression which is somewhat out of place when talking about religion. It is an everyday expression. And wisdom requires that we speak to people within the range of their understanding.

How happy I am to hear from the mouth of a Catholic this phrase: Unity of Religions within Diversity.

It deserves to become a sign written in letters of gold and placed above the door of each house of worship."

We must not give up hope. We must pray. God answers the prayers of those who know how to ask.

How does Judaism feel about Unity of Religions within Diversity? Dr. Bernard Mandelbaum of the Jewish Theological Seminary of America, located in New York City, on November 21, 1960, wrote to the writer:

"Your very thoughtful comments on our message, **Choose Life,** have only now been brought to my attention. I was very much moved by the sensitivity in all that you have to say. Certainly, I think that the general thesis you suggest is crucial. One of the professors at the Seminary talks about the need for Unity and Diversity—in other words, the need for a sense of the common brotherhood of all religious groups, while, at the same time, preserving the unique traditions which each group considers sacred on the basis of its history and experience."

How does the Roman Catholic Church feel about Unity within Diversity? At the present time, the Catholic Church is primarily absorbed in Christian Unity. It believes that Christian Unity is the most important task at hand and that it will, at some later date, consider the problem of *relations* between the Christians and non-Christians. Its position is understandable. The Roman

Catholic Church proceeds slowly with much thought and caution, before making any changes. It is very rational in its actions and in its attitudes.

We are, however, losing a great deal of valuable time in deciding what affirmative cause of action must be taken by religion. The opponents of religion are not standing still. *Religion, like individuals, must accept responsibility for all acts of omission or of commission.* Let us probe the situation deeply.

Although sectional unity is praiseworthy, when considering Christian Unity, must we not, however, consider first the life of organized religion rather than the unification of denominational sectionalism? Is not the life of religion suffering from splintering and lack of proper orientation or goal? *Now is the time for the integration of the entire religious personality. Unity of Religions within Diversity brooks no compromise.*

How do our brother Indians feel about Unity of Religions within Diversity?

Sarvepalli Radhakrishnan, ex-President of India, in his book "Fellowship of the Spirit," published by the Harvard Divinity School and distributed by the Harvard University Press of Cambridge, Mass., gives us an exceptionally good expression of his feelings and ideas towards such unity. He is a person with tremendous spiritual depth. He expresses the hopes, desires and goals of his people. A reading of his book shows in all probability that the Hinduist would be one of the first to cooperate wholeheartedly with Unity of Religions within Diversity. He states:

"The religious tradition of India has been from its early beginnings a distinctive character. It has been vital, flexible and in a state of constant growth. *It has throughout its history been faithful to the idea of unity in diversity.* It respects distinctions and autonomous individualities of social groups so long as they cooperate and fit into the social pattern which has been woven across the centuries."

In reference to the other major monotheistic religions there is no good reason to doubt that they would not cooperate in such religious unity within diversity. *All religions have the realization that all human beings belong to one family.* They are all eager to partake and cooperate in giving expression to such unity. There will be thus a greater realization and fulfilment of truth. Man must practice the truth that God did not make any group superior to another. His love is equally given to all mankind. *His mind is the mind of mankind.* Man will never find peace to the extent where war is forever banished until he understands that the same spirit in any one of us is also in everyone else, that each person regardless of human parenthood is in reality our brother, and that we all have one common father, and that the only lasting and creative emotion is love. No sacrifice is too great in defense of this principle.

In reference to those who are not with us, we must exhibit compassion, humility and understanding. Let us at each opportunity help them in every way possible. *LET INTEGRITY BE OUR TRADEMARK.* When those who do not agree with us are insincere, as at times they will be, let us always return sincerity for insincerity. *With the right spirit, we shall let them see the light, for we are with God.* Let us always show love, humility and discipline, which are Godly attributes.

Equally important with sincerity is the compliance with the "I AM" explanation of the name of God. *In the event we are so blind of soul as not to see the beauty in any religion, we should nevertheless, desist from uttering one derogatory word against it. All religions teach good.* **The one to fear is the person without religion.** Our silence, therefore is truly golden when we thus follow the great gift of HIS name given to us by Moses, which is unchangeable and accurate divine law. (See Exodus 3, 14-15) It is love in action.

When we reproach others we do not exercise wisdom. Wisdom is found in encouragement, in bringing into bloom the good that is in every religion or person. *Love is the exercise of wisdom.*

Let our goal for Unity of Religions within Diversity be one that *always remains neutral, never becoming a church, never seeking converts,* excepting those who do not belong to the Party of God, *never taking but always giving*—the giving of true enlightenment of His laws as the Almighty God gives us the wisdom and the patience to see His laws. Let us always maintain the realization that our knowledge is very incomplete and that we are always fallible. Let us perform our task with love and our joy will be great and our labor nil. Our rewards from our Heavenly Father will be great. Let us build the beginning of such Unity with the great truth:

"THERE IS ONLY ONE GOD AND WE ARE ALL HIS CHILDREN," a part of His spirit.

Let us ask from all the greatest gift that they can give, which is a prayer to our Father, as follows:

THANK YOU O LORD FOR THE WISDOM TO KNOW THAT WE ARE YOUR CHILDREN AND THAT IT IS YOUR WILL TO HAVE UNITY OF RELIGIONS WITHIN DIVERSITY. GRANT US COURAGE, PATIENCE AND AN UNFALTERING DETERMINATION, BLESSED WITH HUMILITY AND MODESTY, TO IMPLANT BY LOVE, SUCH UNITY IN THE HEART OF MANKIND, SO THAT WE MAY LEAVE THIS WORLD A BETTER PLACE FOR OTHERS TO FULLY ENJOY YOUR GIFT OF ETERNAL LIFE. AMEN.

Prayer, when it is properly directed to GOD, is the most powerful force for good on the face of the earth. It gives us correct attitudes.

The fullfilment of Unity will follow.

Communism is here to stay. It, *too, is subject to the universal law of change and is changing.* Let us strive to make its changing always for the better. In the interim, it has not taken the position of granting its people complete freedom. The part, therefore, that Unity of Religions will play in this metamorphosis to maturity of the communists is critical. Only by Unity of Religions can the operation so meaningful to each be performed. This importance cannot be denied.

Reuben Maury, Chief Editorial writer for the News, a New York Newspaper, on January 5, 1962 wrote to this writer the following:

> "The News' editorial position long has been that not only all Christian denominations but all the other religious groups in the world had better form some sort of united front, without giving up any of their individual views, against Communism."

and again in an editorial in the newspaper dated September 30, 1963, stated:

> "It follows that genuine religionists of all kinds better form some sort of united front against communism before it is too late. The faiths have better hang together or they stand a fair chance of hanging separately at the hands of Khruschev or some successor of his."

Only through Unity of Religions can the above be carried out. Pope Paul VI, as the head of the Catholics, and other leaders of the monotheistic religions have the responsibility to religion and to the world to aid and cooperate by every means at their disposal so that we can have Unity of Religions within Diversity. *Unity can only come within Diversity (without uniformity). There is great strength and wisdom in diversity.* A cable with many strands of single wires holds a mighty bridge. One solid cable cannot be used.

Militant communism is strongly motivated. Some communists have become Catholic priests, others Buddhists, and no doubt many of them are found in other religions. The communists rightfully believe that it is very important to know exactly what is going on in all places and at all times. No one can deny that these factors are of tremendous importance. *It pays to be learned, vigilant and well informed.*

Russia now appears to be bending in the right direction. Its attitudes may be changing. Its leaders believe in the fallibility of man and that all men can learn from one another. The Russians are further convinced that man should help man. These beliefs are very good. They will, it is hoped, in time also believe in the Everliving God. *Until they believe in God, it is foolish to trust them.* China, on the other hand, is devoid of the progress made by the Russians and believe in the use of force. Its leaders are playing God and they too require eternal watching, and spiritual enrichment. We may be able some day to reach them through Unity of Religions within Diversity. Perfect love can pierce all barriers. *There is hope,* when their leader, Mao Tse-tung states:

"LET ALL TROPICAL FLOWERS BLOOM TOGETHER, AND THE NATION AND THE WORLD WILL BENEFIT."

It signifies a yearning to be a member in good standing with the rest of humanity.

What should be our attitude toward the communists? The dyed in the wool communist is barren of proper theological knowledge. He needs enlightenment. He has become a non-believer in part, because of his indoctrination and the hypocrisy of many so-called religious men. This is very understandable. The communists, however, are attempting to put in action by enslavement and revolutionary means "Atheistic Christianity." **Man was born of God to be free.**

We must be courageous and patient. Let us emulate God in this very important attribute. *The only good method of completely destroying our enemies is to make them team-mates.*

It is one of the great miracles that man can perform. *The greatest general in the world is the one who can win the battle without the loss of one soldier.* The communists need understanding and spiritual nourishment in order to fill the voids that they have created in their attitudes and thinking. *We, too, however must change some of our attitudes and ideas in reference to our Free Enterprise System. It can stand a great deal of correction.*

Communism is the result of a volcanic complaint which erupted into a revolution. It is a social reaction to economic injustices. Let us always remember the sobering wisdom of Ralph Waldo Emerson, a great literary artist and unitarian denominational theologian, who said:

"REVOLUTIONS NEVER GO BACKWARDS."

We can learn from the communists and they can learn from us. They need growth and so do we. In the interim they need us to find themselves. They need us and our knowledge to feed their people. We must all be convinced that no nation or any one religion can rule the world, that each must cooperate with the other, or else perish. We can in truth state "That there is no problem on the face of this earth that does not have a good solution." *In fact the solution is always present before the problem arises.* Problems are essential and will always be a part of life. Problems are in reality challenges and an opportunity for growth. *Life would be barren without problems.* The good solution is always present. What is the best solution? The best solution is the solution that generates the most love. If it does not generate the greatest love we have not found the correct answer. Let us look, see, hear, think, stop and then act. *The right answer is always there, the question is to find it, and to know when we find it.*

One of the finest acts of turning the Russian communists into the sphere of team-mates, was in the sale of our surplus wheat to the Russians. It was the correct thing to do. Why? We are following the principles of Justice laid down by Christ, not by lip service but by action. It is the principle of the Sermon on the Mount in action. Our enemy needed food and we furnished it. Did we take the correct action in making them pay for it? This was again proper and intelligent in all respects. You help make your enemy a good team-mate when you make him self reliant and self sufficient. We took gold in payment of our wheat and thus decreased the amount of money that the Russians could use for armaments. We gave them food instead of bullets and proved to them that we are not "revanchists" although our physical and spiritual muscles are strong. *They in turn showed us their appreciation by prompt payment and also by changes of attitudes.*

In turning enemies into team-mates we are increasing the potential of a world to live in peace. *By our examples we shall teach them.* We followed the same path of the "principle of non-resistance" with Japan and with West Germany. It works. Let us be forever diligent, however, that they remain team-mates. Deep spiritual development cannot be accomplished in one, two or three generations. *It takes time to eliminate spiritual poverty and for truth to saturate into the hearts of men.*

Our duty relative to religious unity is clear. Delay is disastrous. When the patient is ill and requires, beyond conjecture, a surgical operation, to debate the pros and cons of the situation is foolishness. To delay religious unity is not acting in conformance with HIS laws. *IN SEPARATION THERE IS WEAKNESS AND IN UNITY THERE IS WISDOM AND STRENGTH. GOD IS UNITY.* Spiritual egoism should not be permitted to warp our judgment or deter concerted action by all of the major monotheistic religions.

Humility is the root from which all virtues spring. The more humble we are the closer we are to God. The more egotistical the wider the separation. Let all religions be the first to possess great humility. *Let us not be "I" specialists.* When we act in a superior manner we clearly show our inferiority.

Let us with humility and with love for each other undertake the task that lies before us. It is obvious what He wishes us to do. The world will become a better world by Unity of Religions within Diversity. Let us strive for ourselves and for future generations to uplift man spiritually so that all men can understand, beyond a shadow of a doubt, that we are all children of God and that every person on this earth has within him His immortal spirit. This spiritual unity among man transcends and is greater than any other relationship between individuals. It is the link that makes us all one family. **Unity of religions within Diversity is akin to the stitching that holds a book together so that it forms a singular object, a book.** It then has order (harmony) and thus becomes the means for the preservation and dispensation of knowledge that will insure mental health.

Let us repeat the prayer of ages so that we may possess one of HIS important attributes—COURAGE.

GOD GRANT US THE SERENITY TO ACCEPT THINGS WE CANNOT CHANGE, COURAGE TO CHANGE THINGS WE CAN, AND WISDOM TO KNOW THE DIFFERENCE.
St. Francis of Assisi

Courage is one of the great spiritual values.

It takes a deep, reflected and sincere love of God, for one to have great admiration for all of the various religions of the world *Only the eyes of love can see the actual beauty that exists in the most barren of landscapes.* Genuine love is always the propelling and catalytic force that brings out the best into reality from all those with whom it comes into contact. When the worker labors with love, his joy is immense and his burden is as light as a feather. *The secret of happiness is liking what we do as well as doing what we like.*

Only through Unity within Diversity can we have a refine ment of religion. Such a unity will aid greatly to reduce mate rially the impurities that do exist in religions and relax the tensions among people. Religion will then become the cohesive educating force by which all men will come closer together and to God. Religion, instead of a separating force will become as it should be, a unifying spirit among all people in the universe. The greater the spiritual development of men, the better the world and the higher will man ascend along the spiritual ladder to his Creator.

True security is found in spiritual wealth. All of the great prophets were spiritual millionaires. It is far better to be spiritually rich and materially poor than materially rich and spiritually poor. When we have the combination of spiritual wealth and material wealth we have a tremendous potential to uplift man to the higher divine spheres. As was stated in St. Luke, Chap. 12,15.

> And he said to them, "Take heed and guard yourself from all covetousness, for a man's life does not consist in the abundance of his possession."

The grave danger that delays us in the achievement of Unity with diversity is Spiritual Egoism. This is pride, self will, a false sense of security and is an estrangement from God. It is the cancer of the spiritual world and the paralyzing block in man's ascendency. Our will should be attuned to HIS will, which is the will that controls the universe.

Some of the strong monotheistic religions are Hinduism, Christianity and Moslemism. The Moslems are for Unity of Religions within Diversity. The Roman Catholic Church has, by the Grace of God, the intelligence, the organization and the finances and thus *a sacred responsibility* to the other monotheistic religions to help bring into reality, religious unity within diversity.

Divisions between religions make them very vulnerable to militant atheism and materialism. This disunity thus makes religion an impotent force against the hordes of Communism, materialism and hate, with all their destructive results. It gives aid and comfort to our enemy (our lost brothers).

"But he seeing their thoughts, said to them: Every Kingdom divided against itself is brought to desolation and house will fall upon house."

St. Luke, Chap. 11,17

"Two are better than one: they get a good wage for their labor. If the one falls, the other will lift up his companion. Woe to the solitary man! For if he should fall, he has no one to lift him up. So also, if two sleep together, they keep each other warm. How can one alone keep warm? Where a lone man may be overcome, two together can resist. A three-ply cord is not easily broken."

Ecclesiastes, Chap. 4, 9-12

UNITED, "THE PARTY OF GOD" WILL STAND, DIVIDED IT MUST FALL. THE FREEDOM OF CHOICE IS OURS. (See Wisdom of Sirach Chap. 15, 11-20).

The need for Unity of Religions within Diversity is known to the Vatican. Their file #55/60 states the need for such unity. The prayer for such unity is common to all of the world's monotheistic religions.

"A Prayer for a Better World," * reads as follows:

O HEAVENLY FATHER, you have given us eyes, but we do not see; you have given us ears, but we do not hear; you have given us hearts, but we do not feel; and you have given us minds, but we do not think. Grant us, O Lord, the wisdom and the patience to know Thy laws and to live according to them, so that all things may be done on earth as they are in heaven. Amen

Man makes the error in making the things he can see visually the most important. He often states that seeing is believing. This

---

* A copy of "A Prayer for a Better World," beautifully handlettered and framed under glass in 12"x15" natural oak frames, can be obtained from the Conception Abbey Press, Conception, Mo., at a cost of only $5.00. It has the imprimatur of the Catholic Church, and was written by the author.

error is due to lack of knowledge not only of spiritual law but also of the various sciences. Man cannot see the various waves in the atmosphere. He cannot see X-rays, yet X-rays show the bones in the human body and have been a great boon to mankind. Man cannot see electricity, yet no one can deny its great power and benefit to mankind. *Why then do we fail to realize that the invisible is far more powerful than the visible will ever be?* We do not mean that eyesight is not one of God's great blessings given to man; we mean that we should not use the eyes alone to see. When we use the eyes alone and are barren of faith, we enclose all we can see by a stone wall and an iron fence. We narrow our vision to a tremendous extent. Hence the first line of the prayer. When we do not use the ears to hear, again we narrow our reception and perception. The same is true with our mind. It should always be the receiving and reflection of the divine mind.

When our knowledge is concentrated on HIS laws, *we then tap the spiritual oil well.*

When we seek wisdom and patience to know His Laws (Divine Law), we seek to know His will (Proverbs 1-5). To follow God's laws is to love God and humanity with all one's heart, body, mind and spirit. Let us therefore, have courage and strength, and by continuous prayers and action put into reality, before we pay too great a price, HIS will for Unity of Religions within Diversity. *IT IS BETTER TO BE ONE HUNDRED YEARS TOO EARLY THAN ONE DAY TOO LATE. LET US NOT LEAVE TO THE FUTURE GENERATIONS THE HERITAGE TO REBUILD THE "PARTY OF GOD" ON THE ASHES OF OUR MISTAKES.* Let us pray, like King Solomon, to our Almighty, All-loving and Everliving God, for an understanding heart, for such understanding is true intelligence.

Heaven is here on earth. The earth is a veritable paradise. *It becomes a hell when man is bent on his will* and acts in contravention of HIS laws. Man was not given dominion over man.

God, in His wisdom, reserved that right. *Man is born to be free and no person is so superior to another that he many enslave his brother.* The purpose and goal of enslavement is economic exploitation. When this occurs, man looks upon the other individual as a pawn, as a means and not as a human being of co-equality in the eyes of our Father. His vision is distorted. When our will coincides with HIS will then "all things will be done on earth as they are in heaven." The earth is the abode of both God and his children—man. This brief explanation is given in order that the "Prayer for a Better World" may perhaps be better understood.

God needs man for the expression of His will, to make this world the world it really is. Man without God is hopeless and completely lost. Let us forever pray to our Heavenly Father who is always as close to us as we are to ourselves, that Unity of Religions within Diversity becomes a reality sooner than we think. Man will then become the true brother he actually is with all his fellowmen. *Prayer should always be followed with affirmative, bridled, constant and intelligent action towards the achievement of HIS will.*

The seed of any movement to carry out the will of God, should be planted in virgin soil. The virgin soil is the plastic mind of youth. We cannot start too young. It is a work that belongs to the generation that is just born and to all of the future generations. (Matthew 9, 16-17)

Although the theologian is one of God's great teachers, he too must come to the realization that God is Progress and that He cannot close the ends and make the waters stagnant. *Religionists must always be openminded and vivacious.* God always is making His children better and we should work in harmony with God's spirit. Only through Unity of Religions within Diversity will man come closer to his eternal quest, yes a "sense of integration of spirit, body and mind."

Let us remember a good definition of Hell. A boy asked his father, who was a brilliant theological philosopher, "Dad, what is hell?" The father responded, "my son, hell is knowing the truth too late." Let us not make the mistake of knowing the truth too late. It is only through peace and truth that man can better ascend the higher planes of spiritual development. The beatitude that

Blessed are the peacemakers, for they shall be called the children of God.

is one of the fundamental truths for all times.

CHAPTER V

United Conference of World Religions

What suggestions do we have for spiritual unification?

The first law of God is Divine order. The sun never goes on strike. The moon in its regulated course never fails to shine. The stars are always in their place in the solar system. The law of gravity, like many other laws found in the study of physics, chemistry, and other sciences, never fail to operate. They are divine laws. THINK OF THE INHERENT POTENTIAL FOUND IN ALL SEEDS. Such profound order found in the universe should be proof to the most skeptical mind that God's intellect and laws operate this world. Nevertheless, we should always be compassionate and understanding, respecting those who find it difficult to believe. They need education. They need truth. THEY NEED FAITH.

All of the major religions should designate a secretariat, or call him by any other name, to deal with the other major religions. It would be wise to follow the leadership of Pope Paul VI, who has already taken this step. The office of such secretariat should be staffed by spiritualists who are well schooled in comparative theology (study of world religions), and in addition are spiritual scientists possessing a liberal arts education. They would be thus better qualified to deal with co-religionists. They would know each other's religion and thus be in a greater position to co-operate with one another. An arrangement committee for the first meeting of the World Religions could be worked out easily among them. The arrangement committee could do the planning and the necessary spade work required for such a gigantic conference. With present means of communication and travel, a proper site for such meeting can be selected together with the appropriate formulation of "ground rules." The conference should be in a neutral atmosphere and location, where requisite facilities are available and where the beauty of nature and of climate are present.

We cannot have Unity of Religions within Diversity *by extinguishment* of other religions. There is greater truth in the phrase "live and help live" than in the phrase "Live and let live." The first phrase is active, kind and creative, the second is passive, one of not hurting. *We are not interested in not hurting, we are interested in helping. It is love in action.* The involuntary merger of the various religious ideologies would be an extinguishment. It will never meet success as it is in direct contravention to divine law. It is always better to assert ourselves to give *more* than we have received, than to *return as much* as we have received. The baker's dozen (thirteen in number) is filling the cup of love a little more. This is the viewpoint to cultivate.

A standardization of ritual procedure is not commendable. *It would destroy the uniqueness of each religion.* It would standardize form, create monotony and remove beauty. Why cannot we learn from God? What has our heavenly Father done—has He made only one animal, one fruit, one tree? The abundance of variety of plant life would fill volumes. Flowers are of every conceivable color and shade. What a dull world it would be if there was only one flower with no variations. An orchestra composed only of violins cannot compare with a philharmonic symphony orchestra. When the various musical instruments are harmoniously blending their music, we have unsurpassed beauty. When the various flowers are prepared by an artistic arranger, we again have sights which please all who can see.

The beauty of the various rituals should be maintained. Variety has its place in the universe.

"Order in variety we see; though all things differ, all agree."
Alexander Pope

Our different faiths would be destroyed by any standardization. We are ignorant of other religions because of our failure to visit, stay, hear and learn from other religions different than our own **How can you possibly know the joy of any religion if you do not understand or come in with an open mind and earnestly try to appreciate it.**

> "In many theological institutes both in the East and in the West, the students grow up in profound ignorance of the other religions which if they are presented to them, are done only in gross caricature. They are full of polemics and apologetics. By such a treatment the secret of an alien religion is missed and its genius outraged. By getting the adherents of different religions to work together in a spirit of cooperation and mutual respect, we will promote appreciation of religions at their best."
> Sarvepalli Radhakrishman
> (ibid-1-2)

The prime goal of such Unity of Religions within Diversity would be to bring into reality the inherent unity of spirit and purpose of all mankind, to ripen the unification of the innate spirit of love and fellowship among all religions, so that it may spread from its leaders to their adherents.

Religions have been at "loggerheads" in reference to arriving at some standardization of a school prayer to which they could all agree. Our Courts, because of the provisions of our Constitution removed this issue from public instruction. Some religions actively participated in blocking approval of any school prayer formulated either by the Clergy or by outside agencies. The reason that some organized religions have taken this step is again because of a fear of extinguishment and the desire for survival. This is a natural tendency. However, all of the monotheistic religions can easily combine to agree on one prayer to be stated at the opening of the United Conference of World Religions, and an additional prayer at the close of it. This will cause the realization, the understanding, the unification that they are all members of the "Party of God." Perhaps prayer in the "Research Council" can be further developed to a point where a unified program of prayer for all mankind may be instituted by all monotheistic religions.

In reference to the ground rules to be promulgated, it is wise to remember always that **we are first what we are as individuals and secondly what we are by vocation.** *Whatever a man may be in character is always his true worth and the controlling feature of his life.* If a man is President, or Pope, or King, or Ruler, his position in life is not as important as what he really is as an individual. No one should try to impress another solely because of his particular station or position in life. With this in mind the Minister, the Rabbi, the Cardinal, the Research Spiritual scientist, etc., whoever may be sent to the meeting of the United Conference of World Religions should come as a human being first and lastly as a Clergyman. He should forget, in his association with his co-religionists, the fact that he is a member of any religious sect or that he holds any particular position in the church organization. He should look upon every person as another human being with the same spirit of the Almighty which is within himself. He should respect our oneness with God.

The purpose of the meeting would be to probe the deep questions of life that confront mankind and to **find honest answers, and** not the **"official" answers of a church,** but the individual frank and honest answers of every leader present. The Pope in his Encyclical Eclesiam Suam—"His Church" which was issued on August 10, 1964, gave certain suggestions. It was heartening to read in his Encyclical that the Roman Catholic Church is ready to meet with other religions in promoting and defending 1) Common ideals of religious liberty; 2) Human brotherhood; 3) Social welfare; and, 4) Civil order.

When we have a meeting of individuals with common interests, common goals, common desires and when the interests are discussed and engaged in with sincerity, and with respect for the other fellow's viewpoints, animosity of long standing fades from view. *Under the broad scope of human brotherhood all religions have a common* ground.

What name shall we give such a movement for Unity of Religions within Diversity. A good name might be "THE UNITED CONFERENCE OF WORLD RELIGIONS." No religion wishes to be put into any position where it may lose its identity. *Religionists have worked hard and long in building their religion and have suffered much persecution. Uniformity of religion is not desirable nor is it a good thing.* It would be error to have one religion. It is not and will never be the plan of God to have one religion. To speak in such absolute terms may be to many a grave error. However, if we research God we obviously note that he has not and will never make two individuals the same. **One religion would lead to tyranny.**

The name suggested does not place any religion on a defensive. It is an open invitation to become team mates in the greatest endeavor of man. All religions would have nothing to lose and everything to gain. Where to meet, how to meet and when to meet can easily be formulated by an accord with the representatives of the various world religions. The first meeting should be a get together meeting so that individual theologians and spiritual scientists could know each other better as human beings. All discussions should be in a spirit of joviality. It should be a happy occasion. There should be a comingling of various groups and not an isolation of each group among its own. Their common love for God should be their bond. This bond is further cemented by bands of unbreakable spirit with the truth that we are all children of God. No other theological concept or truth need be discussed. It should be a religious Feast day. The date of the meeting should be proclaimed by all religions as a great day for festivity and enjoyment for it would herald the day of the commencement of Unity of Religions within Diversity. *It should be the day when the entire world, would not only celebrate, but should forever remember the occasion.* It would be the beginning of a new era for man, an upward step on the spiritual ladder to a higher love and appreciation of our FATHER, the Father of us all, and a great love among all human beings. First, foremost and always it should be a labor of unselfish love—thus one of the greatest enjoyable projects on the face of this earth.

Why should religionists work in secret? Is not the PARTY OF GOD one party? *Can religions preach effectively and sincerely Unity and Peace on Earth and at the same time fail to co-operate with their co-religionists?* Should any spiritual truth be kept from mankind? Do we truly love God when those who should know better make this error? Would we have had the progress in the world if the various scientists had not exchanged information among themselves? **Let us remember that cooperation is love.**

It is obvious that although achieving Unity of Religions within Diversity may be as difficult as placing a man on another planet, both goals some day will be reached. When Unity of Religions within Diversity comes into being, it will be a great instrument for world peace. It will be the union of the spiritual bonds that make all human beings brothers and sisters. It will bring into reality in this universe the prophecy of old.

> "And they shall beat their swords into plowshares, and their spears into pruning hooks; nation shall not lift up sword against nation, neither shall they learn war any more."
> Isaiah 2,4

The work of the first meeting of the UCWR (United Conference of World Religions) should be the formation of a *SPIRITUAL RESEARCH COUNCIL,* composed of spiritual scientists versed in spiritual pursuits from all of the major monotheistic religions. They will produce good results.

It is a well known fact that the most important lessons we MUST learn are those which help us to know more and more about God. Dr. Charles Steinmetz, one of the world's greatest physical scientists said:

> "The greatest discoveries will be made along spiritual lines. Some day people will learn that material things do not bring happiness, and are of little use in making men creative and powerful. Then the scientists of the world will turn their laboratories to the study of God, and **prayer. When that day comes the world will see more advancement in one generation than it has in the last four.**"

The first project of the spiritual Research Council should be a very detailed study of birth control. *It is a major problem facing man.*

The world population is reaching proportions where man is finding it difficult to help every new spirit who is born to obtain a fair measure of happiness. We can complain that this is the result of man's failure to share economic wealth with his fellow man. We can advocate that there is enough food available to feed the entire world, but distribution is faulty. All the answers that man can think of do not help the situation one iota. It is akin to finding a man with a broken leg and our interest is to find out why did he fall into the ditch and break his leg. How does that help? Let us bring the individual back to health and later we can determine the means and ways of future avoidance. *Curative medicine first and preventive action later.*

God gave man part of his divine spirit with all the appendages, including mind, love, will, intelligence, etc. These are not barren gifts but gifts that should be used for the benefit of the entire human race. Our Father did not, in giving us the means of human creation, desire that His spirits be born to suffer needlessly. He gave us this world as His heirs so that we may be happy with Him in this world and also in the spiritual world. *Must we depend on wars to exterminate the flowers of human life?* How foolish! Why can we not have sensibly planned families? Let us leave to the dedicated God-loving medical and biological scientists the best manner available to accomplish the good solution to this problem.

A great paradox of life is that man's best friend is man and man's greatest enemy is man. Fortunately, today there is far more love than hate in the world. We have the sobering influence of nuclear power to insure that there will be no victor if FORCE IS USED AS THE ARBITER OF DISPUTES. *Necessity and intelligence now direct us to use that solution, combined with faith, which generates the most love for the born and the unborn.*

The second project of the Spiritual Research Council, in the writer's opinion, is the study of materialism, the reason and the spread thereof, and what religion can do to halt its advance. Man's economic problems should be studied.

Materialism in philosophy is a doctrine that matter is the only reality and that everything in the world, including thought, will and feelings, can be explained only in terms of matter; it is in opposition to theology and idealism. It is the doctrine that comfort, pleasure and wealth are the only or highest goals or values. It disregards spiritual values and makes man purely an animal, devoid of any spiritual characteristics of His creator.

When materialism has increased to the point where individuals place preference for material acquisition above everything that is noble and uplifting, we can ask the important question— what has happened to education, to love and lastly, what is there about religion which has caused, permitted, aided or allowed materialism to obtain such a stranglehold? As one writer aptly put it

"One of the sickening things about the age of materialism is the way man crawls when money is put in front of him."
Jimmy Breslin, Herald Tribune—6/30/64

Communism has twisted Christianity so as to try to make it an atheistic materialistic philosophy or doctrine. Let us remind the communists that there is no such action as a Holy war. We do have unholy wars. The communists make the error of omitting the prefix "un" from Holy. In worshipping war they are worshipping the false God of War. It is idolatry. War does not come from God. It comes from selfishness and undisciplined passions of man. It is ignorance. It can only lead to ruination. It is in direct contravention of the first commandment of God and of Divine Law. **There is nothing in this world that one might hope to obtain by war that cannot be better achieved by peace.**

Karl Marx was a product of German, French and English influence. His book, Das Kapital, is a masterful analysis of the faults of Capitalism, many of which have been corrected. *Untamed Capitalism and Communism are both extremes.* LABOR AND EMPLOYER SHOULD BE ASSOCIATES. NEITHER SHOULD EXPLOIT THE OTHER. Like compulsory education we need to be *taught COMPULSORY SHARING*—sharing our knowledge, our time, our talents, our material resources and our joys with *all* of our brothers. *If the Kingdom of God is to arrive on this earth, sharing must be an integral part of our lives.* Divine law should control our actions.

In bringing Unity of Religions within Diversity to the world, let us remind the materialists of the words of the Psalmist:

> **"The fool says in his heart 'There is no God.' Such are corrupt; they do abominable deeds; there is not one who does good."**
>
> Psalms 13,1

No one is in greater darkness than the one who does not believe in God. No one is more dangerous than the true atheist.

What should be the third task of the Spiritual Research Council? A great labor is the research of justice. (Matthew 6,33). PEACE CAN COME AND BE ESTABLISHED THROUGH RULE BY LAW.

An Encyclopedia of Jurisprudence can be written wherein the various elements of justice can be researched, discussed and formulated. It would be a means of ready reference. It should be a scholarly and detailed work involving cooperative effort. Man would thus know what good minds feel constitutes justice not only to man himself but also to his neighbor. No man can take care of others who does not take care of his health.

No man can be just to others who is unjust to himself. If a person is stingy and miserly to himself he cannot be any better to his fellow man. God in giving us life gave us a corresponding duty to take care of this great gift to us. **Our most important conduct of life is how we treat ourselves and how we treat our neighbor.**

Justice, as stated by St. John, is God. All inharmony in this world is the result of injustice borne of egoism. All violent reactions (revolutions) are the result of injustice. No revolution will ever be caused by the beneficiaries of love. One cannot truly love who is unjust to others. It is basic divine law.

The commandment "thou shalt not exploit nor be unjust to others" is the result of spiritual research. One can observe that the writer's additions to the original Mosaic Commandments make the Commandments more practical.

Justice can be divided for better meaning into three categories or subdivisions of law, Divine law, Natural law and Human law. Perfect justice, absolute justice, or divine justice are all interchangeable terms. Perfect justice is based and flows from divine law. Justice is immortal. Justice is the highest expression of love. It is dispensed to all by the everloving God. We also have social, political, administrative, distributive, retributive, commutative, etc., justice. Such justice is based on natural and/or human law and is dispensed by man. Natural law is the way man sees divine law. Human law is the human pronouncement of law as found in our statutes and case law. Justice, in its complete scope, is a deep and fundamental study of God. It is a study of love. It puts meaning, understanding and fulfilment to the golden rule. A sadist cannot correctly apply the golden rule. His sadism must be first corrected by changes in his attitudes and by a knowledge and appreciation of truths. Life is a comedy to the optimist and a tragedy to the pessimist, all because of the wrong or right attitude. Truth requires us to think in positive terms and not negative terms, thoughts, words and action.

The next agenda, for consideration by the UCWR is the proclamation of fundamental rights and principles, such as:

1. There is only one God, and we are all His children.

2. The members of each religion have the inalienable right to worship God as they please and the right to hold dear and sacred the teachings of their prophets or those they believe were divinely inspired.

3. Human life is sacred and the Spirit of God is in each and every human being, the nature of which is immortal. Human life being sacred, it shall not be destroyed by man.

4. The purpose of life is to live a good and happy life. This purpose can be best accomplished by knowing, loving and serving God with our whole heart, body, mind and spirit. We manifest our love for Him by our love for all humanity, through good thoughts followed by good words and actions. (i.e. by being kind to His other children—our brothers and sisters.)

5. All problems in life and all conflicts among men, groups and nations have a good solution. All problems and conflicts can and should be solved in a peaceful manner. It is the joy and responsibility of religions to actively participate in the deliberations and actions of the opposing parties in order to bring about truth, harmony and justice. The good solution is always THE ONE THAT GENERATES THE MOST LOVE.

6. It is the mission of religion to teach—to teach His laws by quality education, the most important of which are truth, love, justice and self-mastery. **The best sermon is preached by example.** The greatest good is "unselfish love." It is the goal of religion to raise man to higher spiritual spheres, to help to eliminate illiteracy, ignorance and ideas of scarcity or lack, and to train the young to be dedicated, self-reliant and self-sufficient.

7. Where injustice is being perpetrated by any nation or group, it is the sacred obligation of religionists to courageously speak and act against such injustice and designate how, why and in what manner the injustice is in contravention to His laws and advocate what proper steps should be taken to prevent and stop such evil. Religionists like all other persons, should respect all mandates of lawfully constituted authority except where it is in contravention to Divine Law.

8. No religion shall by thought, deed or action, bring into disrepute or ridicule any of the tenets of any other religion, even though any religion has the indisputable right to disagree with any beliefs. No religion shall do anything which will incur or stir up strife, hate or animosity against any other religion.

9. No religion has the whole truth and each religion has some of the truth and that all men can learn from each other. All the truth known by man is but a mere fragment of the entire truth and thus, that the greater portion of the spiritual sphere, which is unlimited in scope, has yet to be discovered. All religionists should, at all times, keep an open mind and respect the views and feelings of their co-religionists.

It is the joy (perfect love and wisdom's countenance) of religion to serve man, follow His will, not its will; be kind, and not cruel; praise, not condemn; encourage, not degrade; think positively, not negatively; unite, not divide; instill courage, not fear; integrate, not segregate; enlighten, not darken; gladden, not sadden; reclaim, not punish; educate, not keep ignorant; understand, not retaliate; progress, not regress; research, not remain stagnant; aid, not hinder; discipline, not leave untamed; cooperate, not oppose; lead (by love), not be led; create not destroy; be democratic and not theocratic; *be always a part and never the whole.*

In whatever we do, let us always be mindful of the words of Jesus, a great teacher of Divine law, as set forth by St. Matthew:

> "You have heard that it was said, 'Thou shalt love thy neighbor, and shalt hate thy enemy.' But I say to you, love your enemies, do good to those who hate you, and pray for those who persecute and calumniate you. So that you may be children of your Father in heaven, who makes his sun to rise on the good and the evil, and sends rain on the just and the unjust. For if you love those that love you, what reward shall you have? Do not even the publicans do that? And if you salute your brethren only, what are you doing more than others? Do not even the Gentiles do that?"
> St. Matthew 5:43-47

Let us be guided by St. Paul in his wisdom, foresight, dedication, teachings, and example, and in his great love for the Everloving and Everliving God.

> "Avoid also foolish and ignorant controversies, knowing that they breed quarrels. But the servant of the Lord must not quarrel, but be gentle towards all, ready to teach, patient, gently admonishing those who resist, in case God should give them repentance to know the truth."
> 2 Timothy 2:23-25

Ignorance is the curse of mankind. Its main branch is selfishness. Let us avoid, by continuous prayer and with all our hearts, strength and mind, the vices of mankind. (2 Timothy 3)

Let no one aspire to leadership who cannot enjoy being a dedicated slave.

"If any man wishes to be first, he shall be last of all and servant of all."

Mark 9:34

If each monotheistic religions were to love all other monotheistic religions with but a fraction of God's love for each one of us, Unity of Religions within Diversity would spring into reality throughout the world within a very short time.

"TO LOVE ABUNDANTLY IS TO LIVE ABUNDANTLY."
Eric Butterworth

Let us be free from prejudices. *Prejudices are all acquired.* They are the result of wrong indoctrination and teaching. They are not innate. A little child is free from such prejudices. His mind has not been tainted by hate. (See Matthew 18,1-4). Much evil springs from this evil. Let us teach the truth. Let us teach Unity of Religions within Diversity. We thus teach love.

Man cannot be happy until he attains the truth.
Sarvepalli Radhakrishnan (ibid 4)

NOW IS NOT THE TIME FOR THE LUXURY OF POLEMICS OR APOLOGETICS. IT IS THE TIME FOR UNITY OF RELIGIONS WITHIN DIVERSITY OR PERISH.

Let us never quit. *The only failure in life is the one who gives up.* Let us stop our endeavors only when we leave this earth. Our labors for religious unity within diversity will not be in vain. *Our progress and efforts will be stepping stones for others who will follow us.* Let us remember one truth about truth —TRUTH PROPAGATES ITSELF. It is indestructible. It is this characteristic which is the reason for its perpetuation and unfoldment. It lives long after we leave this earth. It is eternal.

CHAPTER VI

The Additions to the Ten Commandments

The original commandments which are found in the Holy Bible are the work of the prophet and law giver Moses. They are set forth in Chapter 20 of Exodus and in Chapter 5 of Deuteronomy.

They have been abbreviated in this book in order to facilitate memorization.

In biblical days they were the supreme law of the land. **Their violations were punishable by death.** Capital punishment was deeply ingrained in the times and also in the thinking of Moses. It was used in the following cases:

1. Against the one who had "the insolence to refuse to listen to the priest or to the judge." A wilful disobedience of a court order or failure to heed the "wisdom" of the priest. Deut. 17,12

2. Anyone advocating or preaching idolatry—the violation of first commandment. Deut. 13

3. A man who does not honor his father and mother. Deut. 21,18; Exodus 21,17

4. Adultery. Deut. 22,22

5. The violation of the Sabbath, by gathering wood on the sabbath day. Numbers 15,32. Exodus 31,12-16.

6. Stealing. Deut. 24,7 (King James Version of the Bible)

7. The person who commits perjury. Deut. 19, 16-21.

8. Murder.   Numbers 35,16-21.   Exodus 21,12.   Lev. 24,17.

9. Blasphemy.   Lev. 24,10-16.

10. Sodomy.   Exodus 22,18.

With the refinement of the moral law, capital punishment has been eliminated, excepting as it pertains to the offenses of murder, treason, kidnapping and rape.   In Russia it has been extended to so-called economic crimes.   This is a deviation from the stand taken both by Karl Marx and Engels, who were strongly opposed to capital punishment upon any grounds.

The Ten Commandments are beautiful gems of moral and divine law and are true guide posts for all men to follow in life. They lead to virtue, peace, justice and harmony.   *The self discipline gained by their obedience, is required, commendable and indispensable.*   They are the yardstick of character.

To make any additions to the Ten Commandments was looked upon by many as improper, impossible and sacreligious.   They appeared to be the last, full and complete word on His laws.   To make any change or changes or additions to the Ten Commandments was felt to be in violation of the Laws of God—the Holy Bible.   This concept of Biblical and Dogmatic theology (a closed mind) has prevented, and impeded man from further ascendency towards our Creator.

It has been stated that the Ten Commandments were written by the fingers of God.   (All fingers are the fingers of God.)   Let no man dare to make any addition or changes to the Ten Commandments.

Man does not like changes.   It takes courage to make changes. Progress will always be achieved by changes.   Change is part of cosmic or divine law.

The discussion and criticism in reference to the additions to the Ten Commandments are interesting.   We shall note how some

theologians look upon the sacredness of the original Ten Commandments as enunciated by Moses and how others have reacted to them. We shall also probe deeply and discuss the additions to determine whether they are true, progressive and creative.
Do they expound Divine Law?

The original additions to the Ten Commandments were published by the writer in England. After the printing and when they were being distributed among various theologians, religious universities, foreign groups, and to various leaders in the United States and abroad, a strange coincident occurred. The relationship existent at one time between Moses and his brother Aaron and his sister Miriam seemed to repeat itself.

Moses was as reported, afflicted with a speech impediment. His brother Aaron was gifted with an eloquent tongue. The two brothers were attached to each other and a like relationship existed in reference to Miriam. One day, however, Aaron disputed his brothers right to set forth that he, Moses, was selected by God to lead the Jewish people. This was no doubt motivated by jeolousy and a refusal to accept Moses as a leader. We find part of the story related in Numbers, Chapter 12, of the old testament wherein it is stated:

> "Miriam and Aaron spoke against Moses on the pretext of the marriage he had contracted with a Chusite woman (a despised foreigner—one not of the tribe of Moses). They complained "It is through Moses alone that the Lord speaks? Does he not speak through us also?"

After the Ten Commandments, with the additions, were circulated, the writer's brother in a loud voice stated—"Who gives you the right to change the Ten Commandments." (We note that they are not changes but additions) The answer as given to the above statement was "Who gives you the right to say that I do not have the right to make any additions to the Ten Commandments?" He remained completely silent.

The theologian who was the first to preach a sermon involving a portion of the additions to the Ten Commandments is Dr. Floyd E. George, minister of the Hanson Place Central Methodist Church located in Brooklyn, New York. His sermon on the Tenth Commandment was very interesting, penetrating, instructive and true.

A summary, as taken from notes made at the time, is as follows:

"Exploitation is primarily the lack of love and the use of others for one's own selfish purpose. The individual who exploits, looks upon other persons as a means, as a tool, as an avenue whereby he seeks to achieve something he wants. Man was born to love and not to exploit each other. Generally, you will find that one who exploits others has no true friends. He may have many individuals around him, but none is sincere. As the sun follows night, true friendship for one who exploits others is barren and hollow. (Various Biblical proverbs were cited.)

"Man's inhumanity to man over the ages is the sin of exploitation. (He mentioned Stalin, and other leaders whose sole interest in life was the acquisition of power). Exploitation is also found in the family, where mother or father, or both, exploit their children and vice-versa. Members of a family can exploit one another, using love as the inside track, where the party feels that the person who seeks the request is sincere but there is hypocrisy. Unrequited love is a form of exploitation. We also find exploitation in our social life, where others are used to build up the ego of the individual or the desire for power of the individual. Where others are used to achieve prestige and position, it is exploitation. Where an individual enters a reception hall and goes to pay homage to the powerful or rich individual among the group, it is generally done with the purpose of currying favor. The humble, the meek, the inconspicuous, uneventful person is ignored. Exploitation is the negation of love, since it never gives but seeks solely to receive. To see beauty and to give aid to a fallen individual is to see the beauty of God and do His will. A true Christian can never be an exploiter. He who is truly free from exploitation is one who is unselfish and lives for others. We are all guilty at times of the crime of exploitation. We must continuously pray and guard against it. It is very easy for one to try to use another person for personal gain. Although exploitation is extremely old, it is still modern in its aspects. The racial tensions now existing in our country are due to a great extent to exploitation. Labor in its attempt to secure unfavorable advantage of management, at times, is guilty of the crime of exploitation. Years ago, it was management who was often guilty of the offense and labor the victim. The colored persons' fight for equality is a revolt against exploitation. There are many incidents of exploitation in the social, economic and political life of our country. When we seek a scapegoat for our misdeeds or to cover our crime or guilt when we are at fault, we again employ another method of exploitation. It is using another person to take the brunt of the blame when we deserve it ourselves. It is not in exploiting others that we take the self out of ourselves. The church can also exploit its members and also members can exploit the Church. Two brothers at one time, became ministers of different faiths so that they could keep as their parishioners, patrons of their father, who were members of different denominations. When members attend church to exhibit themselves to others as churchgoers and thus appear to be sanctified, so that they may increase their business, it is exploitation. When the Church uses its members for its own selfish desires for power or financial gain, it is exploitation. Exploitation is one of the cardinal sins of mankind."

This sermon was very illuminating and at the conclusion of the sermon, the Ten Commandments of God, with the additions, were read by Dr. George, before the congregation, together with the joint prayer that they be inscribed in the hearts of all mankind.

Exploitation to a great extent is the cause for communism. The economic exploitations of the people by the ruling class was one of the causes of the revolution. When a person is used for the unjust enrichment of another, regardless of whatever means is used, we have exploitation. There is no exploitation by God of any human being. He unfailingly loves every individual on the face of this earth with equal intensity, impartiality and degree.

The richness of the earth with which He bestowed it in abundance is for all men. When men learn to share with their brothers their love, time, knowledge, wealth so as to be mutually uplifting in the spiritual life of each, we will cease to exploit one another.

There is too much exploitation of sex. This occurs when the creative force in human life is used primarily for pleasure and is devoid of a sense of responsibility. Sex has been given to us by our Everloving Father to be used as the foundation of the family. Man will always degrade himself where it is used for the selfish attitude of abuse of pleasure and sole gratification of the carnal senses. Food has been made pleasurable by God so that we might enjoy eating and at the same time feed the body with the essential food that it requires to sustain life. Does this mean that we should pervert this gift by making the eating of food one of sole pleasure regardless of the amount required to sustain life? What is the penalty for our own transgression and lack of responsibility? Overweight with all of its attendant infirmities and shortness of life. More people in our country have died from overeating than any other reason. *It is our failure to use self-discipline. No man can know God who does not accept self-discipline.*

The young should be taught self control and what constitutes the proper use of the biological organs of creation and the proper use of the other senses. This knowledge should not be left to chance. Some believe that this responsibility is the duty of the parents. What happens when the parents, the school system and the church, all fail to give the young the proper education? *A person who is born is entitled to be taught the truth, as an integral part of his education.* If we fail the young let us not punish them to eradicate the effects of our mistakes. LET US CORRECT OUR OWN MISTAKES FIRST.

The second part of the Tenth Commandment is the phrase "nor be unjust to others." Justice is an all important and embracing subject mentioned briefly in this book. JUSTICE IS DIVINE OR COSMIC IN ORIGIN. The question one must answer is, briefly, why is the treating of others justly so important. What is there about justice that requires that each of us treat the other justly? The answer is found in the result that ensues when justice is given and what follows when it is not given. Justice will always promote peace. Peace is God. There can never be peace without justice. *JUSTICE IS TRUTH IN ACTION.* Is there, therefore, anything more important? The foundation of justice like all other great qualities, virtues and creative forces, is TRUTH. When we treat others justly we reap a bountiful and beautiful harvest. When we treat others unjustly we sow and reap a crop of poisonous weeds.

Let us analyze some of the objections that have been raised against the additions to the Ten Commandments. Let us analyze them, with an open mind to the utmost of our ability. A well written letter, which advocates the view of the biblical theologians, is one forwarded to the writer by Roland H. Hegsted, editor of a magazine called "LIBERTY," a very fine religious magazine. It is a magazine well worth reading and subscribing for.

We should always live by the principle enunciated by Patrick Henry when he stated:

"I may not believe in a word you may state but I shall die for the right that you have to say it."

We should always thank and respect our critics. We cannot help but learn from them. **They may be right.**

Editor Hegsted's letter on February 5, 1964, addressed to the writer is as follows:

"According to your letter, your commandments contain all of the Mosaic Commandments in abbreviated form.

Where is the second, as Protestants number the commandments? "Thou shalt not make unto thee any graven image," etc. This prohibition is not expressed in "Thou shalt not have strange gods before me."

And if the fifth, as you number, means "Thou shalt not have capital punishment," why did the Lord, under the same commandments, prescribe death by stoning for those Hebrews who transgressed the Sabbath commandment? Also the Lord said, "If thy brother, the son of thy mother, or thy son, or thy daughter, or the wife of thy bosom, or thy friend, which is as thine own soul, entice thee secretly, saying, Let us go and serve other gods, which thou hast not known, thou, nor thy fathers; namely, of the gods of the people which are round about you, nigh unto thee, or far off from thee, from the one end of the earth even unto the other end of the earth; Thou shalt not consent unto him, nor hearken unto him; neither shall thine eye pity him, neither shalt thou conceal him: But thou shalt surely kill him; thine hand shall be first upon him to put him to death, and afterwards the hand of all the people. And thou shalt stone him with stones, that he die; because he hath sought to thrust thee away from the Lord thy God, which brought thee out of the land of Egypt, from the house of bondage." (Deuteronomy 13:6-10)

As to the tenth commandment, which you add, is this not braced in the last five of the Ten Commandments, which the Lord said were summed up in this: "Thou shalt love thy neighbor as thyself"?

Really, I have not yet seen a version of the Ten Commandments written by the finger of man that excels in brevity and beauty and comprehensiveness the ten written by the finger of God."

Sincerely,
Roland H. Hegested

In reference to the first statement in his letter we find the query—where is the prohibition of worshiping graven images?

There is no doubt that to worship graven images is a pronounced form of idolatry. In the event one feels it advisable to include such a prohibition in the Ten Commandments, by all means let him do so. All worshiping of strange gods is error and ignorance.

The reason for this objection and statement may be found in the use by the Catholic church of statues of saints. At times we note individuals praying before the statue of a saint as if the saint was God. If the praying before a statue which is a carved image of a person is for the purpose and with the intent to pray to this individual for any purpose whatsoever, then Editor Hegstad is correct. Perhaps it might be better judgement to omit any statues from a place of worship so that this error may not occur. However, if the purpose of the statue is to hold out as a good example the particular life of the individual involved as being exemplary and one that was wholeheartedly in the service of God, there is nothing wrong. Do we not have statues of our great heroes and presidents so that our citizens may remember their good works?

In reference to the response to the Tenth Commandment the query is made whether or not it is summed up in the commandment "Thou shalt love thy neighbor as thyself." This is a wonderful complement from all angles. In the first place, we have a good deduction that the Tenth Commandment is the summing up of the great commandment to love one another. To tell a person to love your neighbor as yourself requires instruction on how this can be accomplished. The commandment of love is as old as religion itself. It has been stated by various religions in different ways. Despite this commandment men have failed to treat each other justly. They have continuously exploited one another. Men must be told how to treat each other. *No individual is intelligent who exploits or treats another unjustly.* Are not these two factors the basic reason for wars, revolution and upheavals? Is it not a direct product of egoism? Let man know the direct causes of conflicts. Let him know that these prohibitions are part and parcel of divine law. As the atomic table in chemistry was at one time incomplete, divine law, we should always remember, is ever in the discovery. *We must understand that divine law can be researched the same as any other law found in the physical sciences.* When we take the viewpoint that we know everything that we should know about spiritual law, what hope is there for advancement in religion in the face of this cardinal error?

In the body of Editor Hegstad's letter, we note his reference to the addition to the fifth commandment—"NOR HAVE CAPITAL PUNISHMENT," the argument that capital punishment was decreed in the Bible for the innocuous offense of gathering wood on the sabbath.

Why is capital punishment contrary to divine law? By what process do we arrive at the pronouncement of this truth? An inspired deduction was made by George Ryley Scott, well known English author, who stated in his book on "History of Capital Punishment" published by Torchstream Books, London, England, on Page 95.

"The general effect of any widespread type of State-induced killing, whether in the form of war or of judicial punishment, is to induce in the populace generally a vitiated and lowered regard for the sanctity of human life. Any such condition is a potentially dangerous one; it is brutalizing in every sense of this expressively comprehensive term. It follows from this that the aim of the State which lays any claim to be truly civilized, is to bring about such conditions as are likely to reduce to the uttermost limit the employment of the death penalty. **Indeed it may well be said that in the extent to which the death penalty is used lies the measure of a State's civilization.** For in the final analysis the State which needs to adopt capital punishment at all stands self-confessed as having failed dismally in the promotion of those social conditions which should constitute the first, the basic, and the most important aim in government."

God is life. In every individual there is the spirit of life. *Man is the Temple in which there is God. God dwells in man.* There is a oneness in each individual with his Creator. Man is part of the infinite. When man executes man under the pretext of Justice, he destroys the Temple in which God dwells. **Capital punishment is man's negative idea of justice.** It is, as stated by George Ryley Scott, **"Murder masquerading as justice."** Capital punishment is plain murder. Life imprisonment would be by far a more accurate form of action by the state toward those who commit murder.

Authority is found in three important spheres of human relations. The highest and the supreme basis of authority is *God*. The perfect order in the universe and in the world as we see it is the clear attestation of the presence of our Father in all life and matter. *He loves us and we should love him by loving all His children.* The second important form of authority is *government*—the society under which we are governed and live. Without authority there would be chaos and anarchy. The next form of authority centers around one's *parents*. Parents have the authority and the sacred responsibility over their children to bring them to maturity by love, example and discipline.

When the example given by any of the human forms of authority, the government and parents, is cruel, vicious, vindictive, barbaristic, and retaliatory, spiritual progress is nil. **Does government expect that the young refrain from killing, when the example given by government is the most premeditated and senseless of any murder that can be committed?** Does an action which is wrong become right when it is committed by a greater number of individuals? If one makes an error in addition, is the same error not an error when made by an organized or collective group? Is there any sane distinction? Is not capital punishment pure retaliation and nothing else? The only deterrent to crime is the knowledge by the possible offender that he will be quickly apprehended and his chances to escape are practically nil. Capital punishment has never been a deterrent and never will be. Let us be realists.

The environment in which we grow, live and develop has a tremendous influence and impact in shaping the future life of any human being. Our teachers, our parents, our form of government, our society, our mores, our friends, make us what we are. Let us try in the best manner we know and with sincere dedication help to make the environment for the future generations a good one. Let us completely eliminate Capital Punishment throughout the world.

Life is sacred and to extinguish human life by capital punishment is in contravention of divine law. It will always brutalize the people and the nation that uses it. Let us advance courageously in the knowledge and advancement of spiritual law. Let us not accept as valid what is clearly wrong. LET US COMPLETELY ELIMINATE HUMAN SACRIFICES FROM THE PAGAN ALTARS OF MAN.

Let us love God, with all our hearts in body, mind and spirit, uprooting from all mankind, the negation of His laws. We can never create human life in the chemical laboratory. Let our justice be patterned after divine justice as God gives us the wisdom, the intellect and the patience to see His laws, so that we may apply them to this earth and thus make the prayer "Thy Kingdom come, Thy will be done, on earth as it is in Heaven," come nearer to man's realization. Man will come ever closer to bring the true spiritual world on earth when he establishes divine law among men.

The additions to the Ten Commandments make them realistic and modern and are the means of man's ascendency closer to God. It is the fostering of man's love for one another and will greatly help to bring the brotherhood of man under the Fatherhood of God.

Men are born to love one another and not to use, abuse and destroy each other. Money was made to use and not to be loved. The truth of this statement is embodied in the Tenth Commandment. Man must realize that killing or mass murder (War) is not God's solution to any of man's problems. Man must realize that life is sacred and no one has the right to kill. Man's recognition of the divinity and the oneness of each person with our Heavenly Father will be the great means of humanity ascending closer to the Kingdom of God. The Tenth Commandment places in action the commandment of Jesus to "love one another," and the wisdom of the "Sermon on the Mount."   The language is clear so that the young mind can grasp its significance.

The final proof relative to the existence of any divine law is to observe what happens when there is a violation of the law. Truth, as has been stated, is self demonstrative. Truth cannot be destroyed and it will always purify the atmosphere.   When we deny the truth or fail to live up to it, we shall always reap what we sow.

CHAPTER VII

Revolutions

"The world is dividing into two camps. One camp believes in God and worships Him through the various religions; and the other denies His existence and believe that religion is a mental aberration." (Amadou Hampate Ba) This division has occurred many times before. Why has such a division re-occurred?

At one time, the Christian religion held complete sway over all phases of human life. It controlled, by absolute power, the temporal and the spiritual life of man. It pronounced truth. It became God. To refute the Church or to disbelieve, question or oppose any of its teachings or pronouncements was to label the party a heretic, to be eternally damned and "the culprit" was punished by severe penalties. Religion was at times the light of the world and at other times, like the pull of a switch, it would plunge the world into darkness. We have had religious wars of great intensity.

With the passage of time, men with great courage fought for expression and recognition in the service of mankind, paying tremendous sacrifices and often with their lives. Physical sciences proved to humanity that science had many correct answers and immensely helped to improve human health and welfare. Life has been prolonged as a result of their many discoveries.

MAN WILL ALWAYS SEEK TRUTH. This desire for truth is a never ceasing inborn divine quest. It is *by this magnet that man is attracted to God and God works out His progress through man.* Nevertheless, religion, despite its setbacks and because of religious revolutions, has gone and is going through various evolutions. *Religion is rendering great service to mankind.*

Due to the errors of religion in the past and because of the hypocrisy of some religious leaders, some men, through various movements believe that they can make better progress for a better world without religion. One of these movements is militant communism. It is akin to seeking the destruction of the medical profession because of a lack of integrity of some of its members. Is there any profession or vocation without this weakness?

Communism is the youngest of the violent revolutions. Previous in time to the Russian revolution we had the French revolution and prior to the French revolution we had the American revolution. What causes revolutions and what are their significance in world events and in world history? To try to know a part of the answer is to understand better revolutions in general.

Most revolutions are caused by man's inhumanity to man. Some of the causes are summed up in the violation of the Tenth Commandment. "THOU SHALL NOT EXPLOIT NOR BE UNJUST TO OTHERS." Let any government permit the exploitation of its people and prevent, by lawful means, the redress of wrongs, and revolutions will naturally occur. Men were born to love one another and not to exploit or be unjust to each other. Men were born to be truthful to each other and not to deceive one another. Deceit brings exploitation. It is the tool used by the exploiter. The violation of divine law causes the effect, the resultant revolution.

When any government refuses to recognize and analyze the complaints of their people and to determine honestly, free from bias, if there is justifiable merit in their complaints, they can expect some day to reap the harvest of what they have sown.

Let us take the human body as an illustration and as an analogy, to understand better the basis of human complaints. A normal individual does not complain of body pains unless there is something wrong. If we have physical pain, we go to a physician to determine what is wrong and how it can be corrected. If on proper diagnostic examination the doctor finds that there is something wrong, he then seeks to determine the best way it can be corrected. As soon as we have a correction the pain stops. The pain can also be psychosomatic and in such a case we know that it is not organic and is the result of the emotions and attitudes of the patient. He may require a good education, spiritual healing, psychiatry, love and understanding so as to eliminate frustrations and permit the proper unfoldment of the individual. His co-operation is always essential. Where complaints in society are selfish, they too require correction. If the complaint is psychosomatic the care and response must be different.

Revolutions always bring change, for better or worse. A change of government is necessary when the government in power does not permit the lawful redress of wrongs because it lacks good laws, good courts and the proper enforcement of its laws. *When the judiciary is so corrupt, that its judges fail to possess integrity, the people suffer.* The country then becomes ripe for revolution. *The foundation of all human power is in the people.* Dictators always live in fear of the people. **He who rules by fear is a victim of fear.**

When revolutions occur there is a tremendous destruction of life and property. Many innocents suffer. It is akin to a drastic surgical operation. A major operation on the human body is always traumatic. How else can the life of the patient be saved? In wars and in revolutions FORCE becomes the arbiter. Thus a heavy price is paid by many innocent people for the ignorance, faults, selfishness and greed of others. If the revolution is a non-violent one, we can be thankful for the intelligence and the wisdom of those in power for the formulation of that form of government that allows changes in a peaceful manner. Laws should be instituted among men so as to give all the people, all the time and in all cases, true justice. True justice is always administered impartially and has as one of its ingredients *a spirit of compassion and understanding.* True justice is kind. It is the rock and foundation of good government.

Men will invariably revolt when the right atmosphere is present, a good doctrine has been set forth and a dedicated personnel is ready. The Negro revolution is a good example.

A Negro having been asked if he was a Catholic, responded, "Hell no, it's bad enough to be black."

Our black brother has for over one hundred years, in America, even though legally free, been treated as a second class citizen. Our black brother is good enough to cook the white brother's meal, good enough to take care of the white brother's home, good enough to take care of his children, often the outlet of the white brother's sexual exploitation, but not good enough to receive the same treatment as all men are entitled to as a matter of divine law. Our black brother is a child of God, with all such benefits, rights and RESPONSIBILITIES.

With the passage of time our black brother found the atmosphere right to revolt, a dedicated personnel, finances, organization and the protection of our Federal law.

The Negro revolution for equal treatment and rights has struck all parts of the world. In time it must succeed, for there is justice in their complaint. They have our Father on their side. THE MUST REMEMBER HOWEVER, THAT THEY ALSO ARE ENTITLED TO POSITIONS ON CHARACTER AND MERIT RATHER THAN ON COLOR. As an oppressed people, they are entitled to certain allowances on their way to equality. They have been denied many things to achieve culture and religion. A crippled man cannot be treated the same as a person who is strong and without any infirmities of body. Justice demands a certain degree of preference because of this inequality.

In time, our black brother will reach a position of culture and of high morality. The day may come, when our black brother may teach his white brother what love and patience truly mean.

He will live by the Ten Commandments and make his light shine among men.

Our black brother should remember that there are many white brothers who have given and are giving their lives, their sweat, toil and money that he might live in freedom with the full dignity becoming a child of God.

Christianity is the product of a revolution. It was a revolt against the injustices and the corruption of the existent Judaic religious hierarchy. It was also a revolution against the tenets of the Roman Empire.

Jesus preached, lived and died for a doctrine that was strange, foreign, treasonable and reactionary for his day. He was a revolutionary figure and possessed tremendous leadership ability. He had the courage of his convictions. He stated that in man is the Kingdom of God. Man, nevertheless has refused to follow his teachings and to heed his truth, not only in the market place but also in the Christian church. The violations of his truths are the causes from which revolutions are occurring. Did he not say in the Sermon on the Mount *"Seek first the kingdom of God and His righteousness and all things shall be given to you"*?

All of the writers and the architects of communism, have been a western product. Their environment was a Christian environment.

We must admit that there was abject poverty, illiteracy and ignorance in Russia prior to the communistic revolution. Exploitation of man by man caused and still causes the subjugation of untold millions. Man has yet to learn the truth "It is in giving that we receive." *To give means dedication to the welfare of your brother, the other humans in this world.*

No person who is not truly dedicated can be a good teacher. To give in all respects is the only way to receive everything worth while. As a result of man's refusal to share, the enslaved felt that the only thing they had to lose from a revolution was their chains.

In the case of communism the enslaved have exchanged one set of chains for another. *Dictatorship is always a system of enslavement.* Man refused to learn from the real master (Jesus), but has been forced to learn from the bitter hand of violent, unrestrained and unprincipled revolutionists, whose sole aim is the possession of power.

Communism places man at the center of the hub instead of God, and materialism as its scepter. It pays slight attention to anything spiritual and fails to exhibit any compassion. It is cruel and ruthless, determined to have its own way. It denies that man is free and makes man a vassal of the state. Communism believes that the state is supreme and that man was born to serve the state. It attempts to spread by bloodshed its doctrines throughout the world. Its desire for power is insatiable and its present success has gone to its head. It rules by fear. *Let us be impervious to fear.*

Communism denies God. It is gross foolishness to deny His existence. No nation that denies God is happy or civilized. Communism MUST be halted and turned back for it rests on false premises. In the long run and at the finish line, "THE PARTY OF GOD" WILL ALWAYS BE VICTORIOUS. GOOD MEN, HOWEVER, MUST WORK TOGETHER.

> LET US ALWAYS REMEMBER THAT ALL THAT IS NECESSARY FOR THE TRIUMPH OF EVIL IS THAT GOOD MEN DO NOTHING.
> 　　　　　　　　　　　　　　　　　Edmund Burke

CHAPTER VIII

Let Us Teach

> "Nor do people pour new wine into old wine skins, else the skins burst, the wine is spilt, and the skins are ruined. But they put new wine into fresh skins, and both are saved."
>
> Matthew 9, 17

MAN'S INHUMANITY TO MAN KNOWS NO BOUNDS. You can still scratch the skin of a professor and find a cannibal. What is wrong?

RELIGION IS BASICALLY THE ART OF BRINGING MANKIND TOGETHER IN LOVING BROTHERHOOD. The word RELIGION is derived from the Latin words re-, and ligare meaning to bind together. The purpose of religion is unification. Its science can properly be called UNITOLOGY—the science of the principles of unity in all its phases. Its theology should be UNITIVE THEOLOGY—the study of the principles of unity as found in God, the universe and mankind, with the aim and purpose of bringing unity (harmony) in and among all fields of human relations. It is fundamental, therefore, that if religions fail to have unity among themselves, they are not religious.

Religion is a way of life, a way of thinking, of acting and reacting, a way of human relations, a way whereby man more and more becomes like our FATHER. IT IS SPIRITUAL GUIDANCE.

Our first concentrated, continuous and persistent step is the education of the young. It is necessary to teach the young why Unity of Religions within Diversity is of extreme importance to man. Man, up to the present time, has failed to achieve the Brotherhood of Man under the Fatherhood of God. Wars have followed wars. God's Kingdom on earth is far from reality. The commandments of Jesus have not found roots deep enough so as to make their teaching a living and potent force. Man has not relinquished the use of war, aggression and exploitation. What is needed?

Education of the young is of prime importance. We can never start them too young. The period from the cradle to pre-school days is the most important one. It is in this crucial period that the future personality is cast. To eliminate hate, exploitation and injustice in the world is a titanic project. Prejudice and hate are the result of indoctrination, given by father to son, from generation to generation and existing over many centuries. It is one infection that seems to attach itself to the oncoming generations with a stranglehold. Man has been powerless to curb it. IT IS MORE CONTAGIOUS THAN ANY DISEASE.

Environment is of greater importance than inheritance. The inheritance is the clay, but the environment is the moulding force by which the clay obtains its form, structure and texture. Our teachers, parents, friends, associates, and mores prevailing in the community, and every other factor constituting our environment help to shape the individual as he is.

We will achieve the unity of spirit that is required to establish the brotherhood of man under the Fatherhood of God only when the monotheistic religions see the importance of Unity and work to achieve unity without seeking uniformity. **How can we achieve the brotherhood of man when those who preach brotherhood are so badly divided?** How can we have unity when there is so much disunity? How can we have unity when religions fail to rally under the banner of God? Do religions have integrity?

How are we going to institute among the monotheistic religions, the sense of the unity of spirit which is always present, but must be given recognition by cooperation as it is expressed in overt acts?

First of all, men must know that everyone in this world is a true child of God. Our relationship and oneness with God must be taught to the young.

Secondly, we shall institute in the educational schools of all the nations of the world, as early as possible, the study of the monotheistic religions of the world. This is a study of comparative religion. The Bible, the Koran, the Talmud, the Torah, the Vedas, the Analects, and many of the other sacred books of the other religions should be used in such a course. These religions must be taught from an objective point of view. What is to be gained from such a study?

Only when we know the other person's religion, will we have a greater understanding of religion and a good basis of contact with the other person. We then will appreciate the ever present beauty in the other person's flower. If all individuals were able to speak one language in addition to their own, which other language, let us say, would be a universal language, would we not have a strong source of contact with the other person? Each additional point of contact that we can make with others will increase the number of friends which we can have. *The more we can reflect to others our Father's love for us, the richer and more productive is our life.* Great will be our harmony and peace. We will come closer to God.

If man was to be asked the simple question which language is the best language, could he truthfully answer the question by any specific answer? Must not the best answer be the language that each person speaks? The language which any man knows is the language that he uses to speak to God. Therefore, that language is the best language. Taken from this important viewpoint, no language is superior to any other language.

To know the other monotheistic religions is to appreciate the different dialects which men use to speak to God. Must we tell

men to forget their dialects and to know only ours? Do we expect
to achieve spiritual unity and His will in the face of this cardinal
error? To fail to seek the truth is to be blind in both body and
soul. To refuse to see the truth is even worse . A study of comparative religion will help immunize the young from the exponents of hate. The young will have a broader education and will
understand the great beauty inherent in all of the monotheistic
religions of the world. *It is in knowing your brother with all his
frailties that you love your brother. We all have frailties.*

In the United States the study of comparative religion is not
only legal but is **strongly suggested by the Supreme Court of the
United States.** *It has the protection of law.* The views of this
court are set forth in a letter addressed by the writer, to James B.
Donovan, a well known attorney and author who is a former
president of the Board of Education of the City of New York. They
are as follows:

> It was with pleasure that I read in the Herald Tribune of
> November 2, 1964, your plea to teachers to instill "moral-
> ity." You raised the query "What can be done within
> proper constitutional bounds to inculcate in our youth
> spiritual values?"
>
> It has given me much pleasure, since my early youth, to
> engage in religious study and in spiritual research. There
> is a trend today where it appears we are going backwards.
> Unfortunately, the monotheistic religions of the world have
> not united, with the result that there are more divisions
> not only in christianity but also in other religions. As a
> result of the divisions instead of having unity we have dis-
> unity with its attendant evils. However, there is a bright
> light that beckons us in a very good direction.
>
> The Supreme Court of the United States, in the case of
> Abington School District vs. Schempp, stated, (374 U.S. 203,
> 10L, ed 2nd, page 844-914) the following:
>
> > "It is insisted that unless these religious exercises are
> > permitted a "religion of secularism" is established in the
> > schools. We agree of course that the State may not

establish a "religion of secularism" in the sense of affirmatively opposing or showing hostility to religion, thus "preferring those who believe in no religion over those who do believe." Zorach v. Clauson, supra (343 US at 314). We do not agree, however, that this decision in any sense has that effect. **In addition, it might well be said that one's education is not complete without a study of comparative religion or the history of religion and its relationship to the advancement of civilization.** It certainly may be said that the Bible is worthy of study for its literary and historic qualities. Nothing we have said here indicates that such study of the Bible or of religion, **when presented objectively** as part of a secular program of education, may not be effected consistent with the First Amendment. But the exercises here do not fall into those categories. They are religious exercises, required by the States in violation of the commandment of the First Amendment that the Government maintain strict neutrality, neither aiding nor opposing religion."

(The above quotation is found on page 225 of the Official reports, and on page 860 of the L. Ed. 2nd reports.)

A constructive subject to study is Comparative Theology. Such a study would embrace the Bible, both the Old and the New Testament. It would also embrace a study of the other monotheistic religions. A study of Comparative Theology would help to make a person a more complete person in that he would have a balanced education. It is constitutional to institute in our high schools a study of Comparative Theology. No man is truly spiritual until he loves all religions. To love all religions he must know all religions, and this requires study. True christianity has no fear of competition.

It would be a pleasure for me to help in any respect possible in this regard. I believe very few theologians would oppose it. To look upon any religion from any sectarian viewpoint is to narrow the microscope to a small aperture. There are many competent and capable men who can be obtained to teach Comparative Theology. It appears to me that if such a course of education was given to the young there would be a greater understanding among all religions—greater harmony and perhaps some day we might have "unity of Religions within Diversity," which I assure you is the prayer of many, many men, and also of many monotheistic religions.

His reply was as follows:

> "This is to acknowledge receipt of and to thank you for
> your very kind letter of November 4, 1964, with respect to
> my statement to the Catholic Teachers Association on No-
> vember 1, 1964.
>
> I am distributing copies of your letter to the other members
> of the Board of Education and to the Superintendent of
> Schools.
>
> I will communicate with you with respect to whatever
> progress may be made within this area."

We serve God when we teach the young the other person's
religion in order that we may help to immunize the man from
prejudice. We must teach the young in ways that foster and
generate their inate energy of love to find expression towards
others. The young have too long been indoctrinated with hate
in divers way, each purpose stemming from an egotistical motive.
Unless the young are taught "comparative religion," there will
always be great divisions between individuals.

Religions should collectively be interested in the acquisition
of truth and the dissemination of truth, not only to their followers
but also to their co-religionists. If a religion is primarily interested in the service of God, it will seek to teach, to all His children, truth and love. Truth and love are inseparable companions.
You cannot have one without the other. St. Paul emphatically
stated *"Love rejoices with truth." Love can only rest on the
foundation of truth.*

We must spread the study of comparative religion all over
the globe. Unity will require time, persistence, faith and good
works. Let us never run out of faith and good works. In this
manner, we will achieve the goal of religious unity within diversity. We will find open hearts in the monotheistic religions.
Long and deep probing has been done to know that unity within
diversity will be accepted by the great majority of the present

monotheistic religions. Let us attempt by all means possible, consistent with truth, to start the teaching of comparative religion as early as possible. Let each religion teach from an impartial, loving and objective point of view. There is so much likeness among the monotheistic religions, that it is foolishness to ridicule or disparage any differences.

We cannot bring religions together by showing how they vary. To point out adversely the differences is to spread disunity. WE SHOULD RESPECT AND LOVE THEM FOR THEIR DIFFERENCES. It is this difference which makes each monotheistic religion unique and beautiful. *It is this slight difference which gives each of them a distinct flavor.* THANK GOD FOR THIS DIFFERENCE.

God has made man, each with different talents. UNIFORMITY IS NOT THE WILL OF GOD. Unity WITHOUT uniformity is the will of God. We have lost the appreciation of the beauty of the monotheistic religions by our zeal to make the world a Christian World. This is spiritual egoism.

Let us with integrity and dedication accomplish our task. We fool no one but ourselves when we are insincere. As Abraham Lincoln said "We may fool some of the people some of the time, all of the people some of the time, but we will never fool all the people all of the time."

Let us go everywhere with open arms and spread the truth, the truth of Unity within diversity. We should always be careful not to prefer one monotheistic religion to the others. *Strict impartiality shall forever be ingrained in our hearts and in our spirit, for we know that it is also ingrained in the Spirit of Him who sends us.* LET US NEVER BE DISMAYED OR LOSE HEART. Greater and more dedicated men will follow our example and will understand the need for Unity within Diversity and make it a reality.

Men know when you are attempting to spread love among the human race. They will flock to hear you. Do, as found in the wisdom of Chinese culture, "Let all save face and *break no one's rice bowl."* NEVER SEEK TO BE A CHURCH. NEVER SEEK TO TAKE EVEN ONE CONVERT FROM ANY RELIGION. SEEK TO SPREAD LOVE FOR ONE ANOTHER AND THE NEED FOR TRUTH AND UNITY.

Two theologies which are needed today are practical and pastoral theology. Biblical theology is beautiful when we understand that despite its great beauty, wisdom and truth, it is a product of inspired minds and has man's imperfections. IT IS THE HISTORY OF MAN'S ETERNAL QUEST FOR OUR FATHER.

RELIGION MUST SERVE MAN AND NOT MAN SERVE RELIGION. There is a tremendous void in religion. Like a vacuum it requires fullfilment. Nature abhors a vacuum. This religious vacuum is crying for leadership. THE UNITED STATES OF AMERICA MUST TAKE SPIRITUAL LEADERSHIP IN THE WORLD. If it fails to do so, it will surely meet and suffer the same fate as the Roman Empire and other great empires and countries before us that have faded into oblivion.

No nation which practices idolatry can long exist. It cannot stand. It is opposed to God. Existentialism, communism, so called humanism, materialism, or any other ism making man the center of the universe, is playing HAMLET with HAMLET left out. THEY ARE PLAYING GOD WITH GOD LEFT OUT. As a result of this false thinking, man denies authority, fails to have compassion and humility, and moral degradation follows. When we deny our creator, by our own error we shut off His love and bounty. We become cruel. When men are sincere in seeking truth, unknown to themselves they are seeking God. Such men, at times, deny God because of their scant knowledge of God. This is also true of many so called intellectuals.

We need good and dedicated leadership not only in religion, but also in government. We need men who know spiritual truth to take the helm. Are we interested only in wealth? Let us remember, "What does it avail one if he has all the wealth of the world and does not have integrity—GOD?" Do we feel that these are idle words? Do we feel that OUR FATHER is an Indian giver, that He would give us life and His spirit and later take it away from us? Life is of the spirit and it is eternal. **The kindness of God is as vast as space and as eternal as time.**

Let us make our country rich in spiritual wealth. Faith will pilot our ship to the shores of safety, peace, courage, contentment and joy. Our light will then truly illuminate the world in the "Brotherhood of Man under the Fatherhood of God, through the Brotherhood of all of the Monotheistic Religions of the World."

CHAPTER IX

His Will

**The only place God is absent is in the
heart of the proud person.**

A book of this type could never be complete without a chapter
as to what constitutes GOD'S WILL.

It is not easy to know HIS will. The great error made by
man and those in power is the failure to determine within a fair
degree of accuracy as to when an action is the human will, and
when it is God's will. Men in position of power, before making a
very decisive act affecting humanity, **should inquire and consider
well what people think,** take counsel with many experts in the field
in which the decision is to be made and consult with spiritual
scientists.

God's will can be determined if we research the problem
from a good rational analytical view together with the contact of
our heavenly Father by prayer in the silent hour. Man's will,
however, can be ascertained through the understanding as to
what constitutes egoism.

Egoism is man's expression of man's will. The egoist is the
true "I" specialist. There would be no war, no hell on this earth
if self will was eliminated. There are two words in reference to
self will that are often used. They are egoism and egotism. What
is the difference between the two? Webster defines them as
follows:

Egoism: The tendency to be self-centered, or to consider only oneself and one's own interest, selfishness. Egotism, conceit. Egoism and egotism are terms used interchangeably, but egotism is generally considered the more opprobrious term. (reproachable)

In egoism, we have the individual attempting to become the center of the earth. EGOISM IS THE RESULT OF IGNORANCE. It is man attempting to be God. The egoist is an atheist. The real theists put God, where HE is—in the center of their hearts, thoughts and the universe. The theist knows, as a child of God, wherever he is, God is. He knows that the spirit or life of God is in each of us and all of us are His children.

Egoism can find many subtle ways of sticking its ugly head into view. Everyone of us has to be on guard that we do not work on others by the use of our will. For this reason *the second thought is very important before we act.*

Egoism can be divided into various classifications. They are as follows:

1. **Individual egoism**

2. **Collective egoism**

3. **Spiritual egoism**

4. **Carnal egoism**

5. **National egoism**

6. **Racial egoism**

7. **Universal egoism**

INDIVIDUAL EGOISM

Individual egoism has the following traits, common to all of the others. These traits are:

1. *Falsity.* The egoist uses lies and deceit. Edgar Hoover, in writing about communism, labelled it correctly when he called his book "Masters of Deceit." The egoist is one who does not use the truth. Lies are his stock in trade. He seeks to have his will DOMINATE THE ENTIRE SITUATION. To the egoist his will is the CENTER of the stage. He is not concerned with the divine will. Obviously, therefore, his chief fault and error is found in lying. In his dealings with others, subterfuge, lack of integrity, chicanery of every type and manner are his methods of operation. He has only one goal—that "my will be done and not His will be done." One can expect stealth, immorality, lack of character, dishonesty, and the violation of the Commandments, in the achievement of his goal. He does not consider God, for he does not believe in the Everliving God. The all important concern is his self concern.

2. *Irresponsibility.* The second great characteristic of the egoist is his irresponsibility. He is not concerned with how his actions affect others. He does not consider the effects of his actions upon other parties. His only interest is how his actions affect himself. His love is inward and not outward. If his goal is world conquest, man is but a tool in his machinations. He lives for himself. Tertulian, an early religious writer and ecclesiastic aptly stated:-

"The selfish person confers the world a favor when he dies."

The egoist is a parasite. He takes much from the world and any giving on his part is purely accidental.

3. *Super-sensitivity.* The egoist is vain and is not able to take criticism in the correct manner. He is easily offended and hurt. He thinks so much of himself so that if his image of himself is any way lowered, his reaction to the situation is one of anger,

retaliation, suspension of contact with the "guilty" party and general antagonism. He does not roll with the punches. He cannot accept criticism as a revealing force as it may be the truth. He does not look upon his critic with favor. He cannot see the tremendous value in criticism. His attitude is a wrong one. He is puffed with praise and floored by criticism. He likes "yes" men.

4. *Obstinacy.* The egoist likes to have his own way, he is a spoiled child. His frustration tolerance is low. He attempts to have his own way at times regardless of the cost it may bring to himself or others. He is unreasonable and does not respond to logic. He is spiritually blind and can see only his particular view of any situation. He is so wrapped up in himself that he is identical with a horse that has blinkers on, he can see only in one direction, his way. He does not consider that the will of others should be taken into consideration and deliberation. He gives no thought to the Divine and controlling will of the universe. He is floating in space, unanchored to any mooring. He is thus very flighty, impulsive and undecided. He is very changeable, swinging with each tide and breeze. He is very unreliable.

5. *Haughtiness.* The egoist shows his egoism, not only by what he says and does, but also how he acts, talks and walks. His mannerisms betray his inner thoughts. Our thoughts control our speech and our actions. The greatest dynamic energy in the world is thought. It is the steering wheel by which man controls and directs himself. If we have good thoughts our speech and actions will be good. WE ARE WHAT WE THINK. It is *the substance* of which we are formed.

What makes any one person have contempt for the views of another? What makes one believe that his or her common sense and wisdom is complete? What makes one feel that he has complete truth? What makes one feel superior to others? The answer is PRIDE-EGOISM. Let man know respect, and love the Infinite and realize that any number is but a fraction of the Infinite, then he may know his true relation to our beneficent Father, the Creator of everything. We can use the following fraction in calculating our knowledge in relation to GOD'S knowledge.

$$\frac{\text{The Human Race—One Billion Trillion}}{\text{God (Infinite)}} \text{(Or any number than man can conceive)} = \text{a little more than zero}$$

When man knows all that he is, all that he hopes to be, and that all joy, wisdom, happiness, and all the benign attitudes emanate from our Heavenly Father, man will cease to be haughty, selfish, greedy and vain. He will be a true brother for he is then a good child of God.

"YOU MAY BE THE CROWNING STONE AT THE CREST OF THE PYRAMID, BUT ITS THE OTHER STONES WHICH KEEP YOU THERE."

Anonymous

6. *Eccentricity.* The egoist always stands out from the group. He seeks the center of the stage in one manner or another. He is a professional credit grabber. He has an insatiable appetite for praise. When a person dresses in such a manner as to clearly show a marked deviation from others we can rest assured that we have an egoist. When he is eccentric by speech or manner we say that he is queer. His desire is for everyone to notice him. It is the subconscious motive for his eccentricity. Centering his life around himself makes him warped, which is reflected in his actions. He is a very poor listener for he loves to do all the talking.

7. *Violence.* The egoist at times, in order to achieve what he wants, when he wants it, fails to have the virtue of patience. In his impetuousness he resorts to violence. Men who have justifiable grounds for the seeking of fundamental justice, and are God

loving, have patience in the achievement of their goal. Most leaders of passive revolutions are experts in patience, faith and in putting into action the principles of non-resistance. *It takes a real brilliant leader who has God as the center of his life, to lead in such an enviable manner that the ultimate goal is achieved without the destruction of human life.* To be a true leader requires a great love of our Father, tremendous patience, reflected wisdom, a humble heart and willingness to be a *real joyful slave for his followers.* He is THE genuine leader among us. The egoist looks for short cuts. He cannot wait. He must see the realization of his dreams during his life time. If a violent revolution will accomplish his goal or goals then by all means he seeks it. How different from the dedicated martyrs. The real leader is *one who is willing to give all that he has, including his life for a world that he may not see on this earth.* He seeks to achieve his lofty goal by patience, preaching, teaching, example, serving, praying and loving all of humanity. He is indeed the devoted servant of our Father.

In speaking of egoism, do we mean to infer that an individual is to destroy his will and fail to express himself? The answer is no. There is a healthy and necessary assertion of one personality. A complete rejection of one's will leads to frustration, unfullfilment and neurosis. The distinction between the egoist and the normal individual is that the egoist thinks only of himself, in total disregard of the rights and feelings of his fellow human being. The egoist is only interested in "What is there in it for me?" The egoist therefore fails to extend to others that measure of co-operation which is necessary, to achieve the teamwork that is required, to place into reality the human relations and the resources which serve the common cause and the brotherhood of man.

A person is not selfish when he treats himself well. He must have an obligation to treat himself properly. One has the obligation to take care of his health. *God has given one life with the corresponding duty of taking care of it.* He has the duty of seeking enjoyment, recreation and diversion. He is entitled to the freedom of labor, to love and to worship.

One should always act with integrity so that he may rightfully have a good opinion of himself. *He should not compromise his character under any condition whatsoever.* To treat others fairly and justly is the mark of a good person. He can look at himself straight in the eye for we cannot fool the person called I. We may be able to fool all of the people but we can never fool ourselves. We know the truth. A beautiful poem that clearly and beautifully expresses this thought is as follows:

THE MAN IN THE GLASS

When you get what you want in your struggle for self
    and the world makes you King for a day,
Just go to a mirror and look at yourself,
    and see what that man has to say.
For it isn't your father or mother or wife,
    whose judgment upon you must pass.
The fellow whose verdict counts most in your life
    is the one staring back from the glass.
You may be like Jack Horner and chisel a plum
    and think you're a wonderful guy,
But the man in the glass says you're only a bum
    if you can't look him straight in the eye.
He's the fellow to please, never mind all the rest,
    for he's with you clear up to the end,
And you've passed your most dangerous, difficult test
    if the man in the glass is your friend.
You may fool the whole world down the pathway of years,
    and get pats on the back as you pass,
But your final reward will be headaches and tears
    if you've cheated **The Man in the Glass.**

                              Anonymous

Thanks is expressed to Right Rev. Monsignor Aloysius C. Dineen, Pastor of the Church of St. Agnes (R.C.) located on East 43rd Street, New York City, for forwarding this poem to the writer.

When we seek economic security and good friends to enjoy, we are not selfish. It is the proper and right thing to seek our inheritance as an heir of our Father. Man is a gregarious individual; he requires the need of other humans for his mental and spiritual growth.

When we center our lives around ourselves we pay a great penalty. What happens? WE BECOME UNHAPPY. We see life through a very small microscope. We lack humility. We separate ourselves from God. We run into trouble. We make ourselves a problem to others. Humility is the understanding of one's true relation to others and to God. Suppose God were selfish and showed partiality to some? Supposing He preferred some of His children as heirs and neglected others? Would we have this earth?

OUR CENTER IN LIFE SHOULD BE A GOAL OF LOFTY IDEAL OR IDEALS. It should center around God and the consideration and rendition of aid to others. It means the contribution of our labor in the increasing of the common warehouse of goods and usable wealth. It means the rendition of services to mankind. It thinks and acts for the welfare of others. It means the love of humanity. It means that "THOU SHALL NOT EXPLOIT NOR BE UNJUST TO OTHERS." It means that you shall be truthful to others. It means that you share and co-operate with others. THE ONLY WAY TO BE REALLY SELFISH IS TO BE TRULY UNSELFISH. Why? It is true character and YOU ARE TRULY HAPPY. You walk with God. Our closeness to God is in direct proportion to the extent of our selfishness. The more selfish we are the further we are from God. The less selfish we are the closer we are to God.

"Selfishness is that detestable vice no one will forgive in others, and no one is without it himself."
                                        Henry Ward Beecher

We are unselfish when we love all of mankind, regardless of race, color, creed or national origin. We not only look upon every individual as our brother *but we treat every one as a brother.* It is reaching that stage of spiritual development where we look upon each human being as a child of God, knowing that our Father is the true Father of us all. When this knowledge is deeply ingrained in our thoughts, words and actions we know that we are near the summit where we reflect His love to His other children, every human being in the world. This love has the main ingredient we call compassion, which is the eagerness, and desire, and the joy in uplifting our fellow man. *There is no room or thought for power, or glory, for you know that these attributes belong eternally to our Father alone and no one else.*

COLLECTIVE EGOISM

Egoism as it pertains to the individual can also pertain to a collection of individuals who band together for various purposes. When individuals gather in groups to accompiish a good end, we have progress, and through teamwork, we have love at its highest expression. Great accomplishments can be made only through co-operation with others. When the group, however, is spurred solely by selfish motives, without regard for the rights and feelings of other people or groups and is desirous of obtaining its own objectives at the expense or exploitation of others, we have collective egoism. It is the attempt of the group to enforce its will on others. Generally it is based on economic exploitation which underlies its action. They are selfish because of the fact that they are completely self-centered and act and behave as if they were the only ones on this earth. They are in need of education and the rejection of their aims which are not conducive to the common good. They need control, re-organization and good leaders and if the same is not possible, dismemberment. Authority of government belongs in the hands of dedicated leaders who truly enjoy being the slaves of their constituents and are very happy to be in the service of our Father. *No man, without true spiritual insight, should ever be permitted to be a leader.* True leadership must have as its foundation, truth, integrity, intelligence, and persistence to seek His will and to put it into action.

A true leader knows how to lead not by power (fear) but by consent (love). Unless a man has the proper foundation, he should never lead. A GOOD LEADER IS NOT JOLTED INTO DIZZY HEIGHTS OF ECSTACY BY THE PLAUDITS OF MEN NOR FLOORED BY ADVERSE CRITICISM. His thoughts are always centered on God. He must also have the indispensable quality of compassion. To err is human, to forgive always divine. The true leader listens and seeks the counsel of others before decisions are made. He knows the value of prayer and in solitude communes with our Father. He is a man who has and continuously seeks divine inspiration. Truth is his stock in trade. Integrity is his badge of honor. Character is his foundation. He walks humbly with his God.

This collective egoism is found in many groups. It is the seeking of more than one's share. It seeks an advantage. Where the group seeks true justice for its members, it has the blessings and the help of our Creator.

SPIRITUAL EGOISM

Egoism has its tentacles in all of human endeavors or action. Religion can be also affected. It has been and is being affected by spiritual egoism. *THE MAIN BLOCK TO UNITY OF RELIGIONS WITHIN DIVERSITY IS SPIRITUAL EGOISM.*

Diversity of religion is good. It is necessary. Without diversity there would be no progress along spiritual lines. PROGRESS COMES THROUGH CHANGE. A healthy desire for religions to seek truth and to serve its members by education and by pastoral and practical theology in facing the myriads of problems in life, is truly noble. It means vigorous mental health. A man who does not know or believe that he is a spiritual being, governed by divine or cosmic law, is very unfortunate. He needs education. Religion serves man through its good works and by means of education. Religion therefore must be free. Every religion should give to other religions the same freedom that it seeks for itself.

When a religion believes that it has all the truth, that it is the only religion where men can come to God, *it centers itself to itself*. It then makes the cardinal error of spiritual egoism. Such a religion fails to help its members; it is bound to be ambivalent for it seeks the expansion of its teaching at all costs and is not considerate or understanding in reference to others of a different mind. *It commits the unforgiveable error of a closed mind.* Where any premise or teaching of any religion is not based on truth, it can be preached for centuries and still rest on an unstable and insecure foundation. Hitler believed that if you stated and taught a lie often enough and long enough it would be believed. Yes, it would be believed by many men but never by all men. In the end anything which is not based upon truth must fade into oblivion. TRUTH IS NOT PERISHABLE.

Religious wars were due to spiritual egoism. Religion used the process of war to enforce upon others its particular belief. It has found that it was mistaken. *Right will always make might.* Right may falter in its fight for recognition and victory, but eventually it must succeed. *JUSTICE UPON WHICH RIGHT IS BASED IS COSMIC OR DIVINE IN ORIGIN.*

On many occasions some religions have been intolerant of other religions. They have denied the freedom that they have achieved to other religions that have sought the rights. This is obviously pure hypocrisy and spiritual egoism. It is selfishness in its highest form.

The chief block to Unity of Religions within Diversity has been and will be Spiritual Egoism. It is due to a false sense of pride, pride of authorship, pride in reference to their prophets, belief that their religion is the best, and that salvation can only come from membership in their religion. It is a failure to respect the viewpoints of others, to engage in teamwork in the many good works that can uplift man in the sphere of human relationship and in the love of God. It is the failure to make God the center of their goal, as exhibited by a lack of love for their co-religionists. Spiritual egoism is found in the failure of religion to love those who do not believe in the way they do. Religions fail to understand that there are many roads leading to God, which roads always blend into the road of Truth as they reach the throne of God. It is within the power of religion to bring man together in the common bonds of brotherhood by joining hands with all of the monotheistic religions in helping to solve the problems of mankind in a peaceful, sensible and cooperative manner. If each monotheistic religion would realize the blessings of teamwork, and understand that *first place belongs now and forever to God and God alone,* it will achieve its rightful place of service in human society. We will then have more good accomplished on this earth than has ever been done before.

Peace on earth depends more on religion than religion understands today. The responsibility for the success or failure of man to live in peace falls directly upon the shoulders of the monotheistic religions. THEY MUST CEASE TO BE AMBIVALENT, LOVING AND HATING AT THE SAME TIME. *Religion must teach the truth and must be based on truth.* It is upon truth that faith, love, happiness and progress rest and depend. Each religion must learn to love its enemies with all of the love that God could possibly give human beings.

Perhaps at all the meetings of the United Conference of World Religions it would be best to have one ritual expressed by an empty chair, directly in the center of the stage. The purpose would be to remind all present that FIRST PLACE is held by our loving Father and no group of humans, nor any living person can take this place. It would be a solemn reminder that all monotheistic religions lead to God, that they must all work together for the common good of man, that they should cooperate with one another in the many, many avenues that can benefit the human race. *Religions have been instituted by God for the service of man, and not man for the service of religion.* Religion should continuously strive to eliminate from its midst spiritual egoism. Let each hear from all the other monotheistic religions any criticisms each has for the other to the point of exhaustion. Let them derive from one another the power to see themselves as they really are and to derive the great blessings of the Almighty God from such an advantage. Let criticisms be mentioned in the spirit of love, in the spirit of brotherhood and with the conviction that each of the religions is but a different dialect through and by which man communicates with God. *Let them work together so that they may know each other better.* Let them pray together so they can worship as members of one party "The Party of God." *Let them work together for peace among men by showing peace among themselves.* THIS IS GOD'S CHALLENGE TO RELIGION. May it have the wisdom to accept the challenge and grow in love of Him. The human race will be the great beneficiary of such action and religion will make the greatest advancement that it has made to date in all fields of human endeavor.

CARNAL EGOISM

Carnal egoism briefly is the abuse of lawful sensual pleasures. Carnal means "of the flesh." It pertains to the senses given to man by our Creator for certain specific purposes and reasons. We shall take the senses of taste and sexual pleasure as the major senses involved. The sense of taste was given to man so that he would find joy in eating so that he may sustain the body. It was given in order to maintain life and to give man the pleasure of taste as to the many and varied foods which are *His gift to us.* Where the pleasure of taste is controlled, we have joy, satisfaction and health. Where we have an uncontrolled appetite we have what is called a "FOOD DRUNKARD." His main desire is a continuous satisfaction of the taste of food; he is irresponsible in reference to what happens where there is overeating. At times he suffers untold misery and illnesses as a result of the over burdening of the body in the digesting of food and in the carrying of overweight. There is a lack of control. There is a lack of knowledge of cause and effect. He needs education. In the same category is the alcoholic. He drinks to excess and dulls his mind, trying to avoid the facing of problems. *He does not realize that our Father never gives us a problem that we do not have the ability to face. He never tempts us beyond our means.* The alcoholic is an escapist and needs spiritual education and instruction in how to face and solve his problems better. There are many places where he can be helped if he desires to be helped. THE TEACHER IS ALWAYS AVAILABLE WHEN THE PUPIL IS READY.

Sexual pleasure was given to man in order that man may find the gift of creation one of beauty. It was given, however, to be used for a definite purpose and not to be used strictly for pleasure. Where it is used for pleasure alone it degrades the individual *for it lacks love.* The relationship between the parties involved lacks the love *that is of the spirit.* Where love is carnal, based on the pleasures of the flesh, it is but an illusion. It is false and will not endure. God in causing man to conceive marriage, gave His children a taste of heaven. The joy of a family, the reciprocal love and loyalty of a devoted partner, in all kinds of tribulations and joys, the union of two spirits in one, make marriage the partnership by which both members achieve fullfilment and expression.

The abuse of lawful sensual pleasures causes the human being to be out of balance. *The spirit and the flesh are at war with each other. The spirit is eternally dominant.* The spirit of God is in every human being. The spirit controls the body. The flesh is subject to, and under the domination and control of the spirit. WE ARE RESPONSIBLE FOR OUR CARNAL EGOISM. The power to harness, subjugate, discipline and control it *is within all of us.* To deny this power in man is to deny free will. It denies God.

NATIONAL EGOISM

National egoism was touched upon in the beginning of this book on the chapter "Causes of Human Conflicts." Where the leaders of any country are so engrossed in taking first place among all of the nations of the world, there will be national egoism and there will be trouble. Man should remember that first place is not reserved for any nation, organization or man. When men under the emblem of a flag seek to dominate the world, they are engrossed in the love of power. Power and glory, like first place, is reserved for our loving Father. Let us put things in proper order so that we may have HIS peace. *Power is not the resting place or ultimate goal of men.* The leaders of any country should, before acting, carefully meditate their moves, so as to insure as humanly as possible the carrying out of His will. Any leader who has failed to have a good education in comparative religion or theology is lacking the education that a leader should have. Where his religious education is along one sectional line only, he will not be able to understand true spirituality. THE PLACE IN THE SUN FOR ANY NATION IS ACHIEVED BY SHARING THE SUN WITH OTHER NATIONS. This is divine justice. Truth MUST be used if we are to deal justly with one another. It is the essential ingredient of justice.

The national egoist is therefore a self centered individual. He may appear to have the cloak of humility. It is mere acting. He is intoxicated with praise. He seeks the limelight and not the desire to let his light shine upon men. When there are attempts on his life, he generally seeks the immediate execution of all those who took part in the attempt. He is extremely vindictive. He does not have the love of mankind that was exhibited by Jesus. He seeks to rule through power. His weapon is the weapon of fear.

No man should permit any other individual to make a door mat of him; no nation should permit any other nation to exploit, deny or take away from it freedom. Men and nations were created to be free and to develop their full potentials under freedom. *No nation has the right to enslave or exploit any other nation.*

RACIAL EGOISM

Racial egoism is the false belief in the superiority of one race over another. It is again an attempt to make a particular group THE leading group in the world. When we have racial egoism we have the attempted exploitation of other races. True leadership is not based on the common link of color, but rather on the unifying force of the spirit. No race is superior to another. No race has the right to exploit or enslave any other race. *Freedom is the birthright of all races.* Where we have racial egoism we will find that its leaders are bent in having their own way, regardless of the costs in life and property. It has all of the faults found in individual egoism, with the added fact *that color is the rallying point* upon which their leaders operate. THINK YELLOW THEY WILL SHOUT. THINK BLACK: THINK WHITE SUPREMACY is their cry. Never do they say, MAKE GOD THE CENTER OF YOUR THOUGHTS, ACTIONS OR LIFE. They do not teach love but *they do teach hate.*

Racial egoism requires more education today than any of the other forms of egoism. It has become a serious problem to the whole human race. There must be more understanding by the individual, called a human being, in his relation to His creator and to each other. There must be the realization that we are all brothers having ONE FATHER who is God. We should refer to the various races as OUR GOOD BLACK BROTHER, OUR GOOD YELLOW BROTHER and OUR GOOD WHITE BROTHER. *We should thank God for the color of our skins and not wish that we were born with any other color.* Most people have some color. *What counts in a man is integrity—character, lofty ideals, and nothing else.*

UNIVERSAL EGOISM

Universal egoism is the composite of all of the various forms of egoism as it expresses itself in human nature. It is the summarization of the quantity of egoism in the world at any given time. It is akin to the chemical analyst who determines the amount of a particular chemical in any solution. *It is the quantitative analysis of egoism.*

There is a tremendous amount of egoism existing today. Man is too self-centered. It is expressed in so called humanism, materialism, communism, existentialism and every other ism that attempts to center man's world around man.

Where do the atheistic err? The answer to a great extent is found in the fact that "THEY FAIL TO KNOW WHO THEY REALLY ARE." *They are OUR LOST BROTHERS.* They do not know the following:

1. That they are children of God.

What do we mean when we say "They are children of God"? What is its basic significance? What are some of the proper thoughts that we should allow to enter our minds when we think or use these words?

To be a child of God means that the life, spirit and the power of God is within us, that we dwell in God and God dwells within us. The strength of its meaning lies in the fact that as His children He has endowed us with great freedom. This freedom is THAT WE CAN BECOME ANYTHING WE WANT TO BE. It is for us to decide what vocation and what type of person we wish to follow or become. If we want to be a doctor, lawyer, dentist, artist, farmer, mechanic, business man, policeman, fireman, teacher or select any other career, we can accomplish our goal. Lack of money or any other impediment may delay us in the achievement of our goal, but we cannot be denied its fullfilment. If our wanting is strong and persistent enough THE MEANS ALWAYS BECOME AVAILABLE. *Our Father supplies the need.* This important freedom of choice is present even if we want to be a prophet or a messiah and thus change for the better the course of the world. God in making us his children fullfils our wants. In addition to picking our vocation, we can also become the person we want to become. *We can be a sinner or a saint.* When we state our ideals and the ones we admire, one knows who we desire to be and the type of person we are becoming.

2. That God loves, cares and provides for ALL of his children. Any failure to receive His love is due to our blocking and not HIS.

3. That we, as his heirs are the recipients of a rich, bountiful and beautiful world, which He made expressly for us.

4. That each of us has His immortal spirit within us.

5. That we are first, last and always spiritual human beings, in addition to being physical beings, and death is but a passageway from the natural world into the spiritual world of our FATHER.

6. That the hell that man creates on this earth is due to ignorance and greed. Our overexaggerated fears and anxieties are due to our blindness in spirit.

7. That failure to see that the world in its majestic splendor and in its divine order is the creation of an ineffable genius, whom we are exceptionally fortunate to have as OUR FATHER. COULD MAN ASK FOR MORE?

IT IS FOR THE ABOVE FAILURE THAT TODAY WE HAVE DANGEROUS TIMES, AND THAT THE WORLD IS DIVIDING INTO TWO CAMPS—GOD AND ANTI-GOD. Where such a cleavage exists demoralization is bound to set in. Man begins to deny God. When man denies God, he denies His laws and their violation brings its own punishment. *When there is no authority we have chaos.*

St. Paul in his second pastoral epistle to Timothy, Chapter 3 clearly pointed out the effects of universal egoism. He stated:

"But know this, that in the last days dangerous times will come. Men will BE LOVERS OF SELF, covetous, HAUGHTY, PROUD, blasphemers, disobedient to parents, ungrateful, criminal, heartless, faithless, slanderers, incontinent, merciless, unkind, treacherous, STUBBORN, PUFFED UP WITH PRIDE, LOVING PLEASURE MORE THAN GOD, having a semblance indeed of piety, but disowning its power. AVOID THESE. BUT THEY WILL MAKE NO FURTHER PROGRESS, FOR THEIR FOLLY WILL BE OBVIOUS TO ALL, AS WAS THAT OF THOSE OTHERS."

It is in the study of egoism, and how it is at war with the spirit that we can determine to a very good degree of accuracy what HIS will is. **Egoism is diametrically opposed to HIS will.** God clearly shows man the way to go. His example is everywhere. His work is obvious. His laws are clear and unambiguous. Let us learn to love each other as He loves us.

An important step, in an attempt to determine His will, is to ascertain and give very grave consideration to what others think about the issue at hand. We should try to determine what is the *common sense* answer to the problem. *A person who does not ascertain, respect or heed what others think about an issue is bound to make many errors.* Let us attempt to answer the question—Why is it important to know the thoughts, feelings and views of others on any matter?

Every human being is of the spirit of God. We are all antennas by which we tap into the Eternal Mind, the God circuit. We are all the inlet of His great gifts. Humanity reflects His love, His intelligence, His wisdom and His fortitude. If a leader does not consider this all important factor in making a determination, can we call him a good leader? As mentioned before, a leader is one who is a "JOYFUL SLAVE." Let no one seek to become a leader, who does not truly enjoy to the fullest the role of a good servant. A true leader is a very unselfish and God centered person, possessed of great love, endowed with character, wisdom and compassion. He is interested in what is best and just for his people, not what is best for him. He does not look for power or glory. The desires of the people are his main desires, their welfare is paramount and their joy is his joy. He is a person who can dispense "SPIRITUAL BREAD." He is a free man, who loves God, with his whole heart, his whole soul and his whole mind. He has a cool temperament in the face of adversity; he possesses self discipline and self control under difficult circumstances. He has the courage of his convictions and is a person with DEEP FAITH.

Another essential in determining our Father's will is to seek and engage the services of competent qualified experts that can suggest good solutions to the problem at hand. No man can know everything. *Experts are men who know a great deal about a little.* When the problem is within their field it is wise to determine who they may be and to engage their services. Selection of experts should not be based on partisanship but strictly on merit. Their views should be given long, grave and the utmost consideration. They have more of the accumulated knowledge of a given problem. To disregard knowledge is to be foolhardy.

We then come to an important step which many so-called leaders fail to follow, thus causing many serious blunders:- to consult men who possess spiritual knowledge. A truly religious individual, as previously mentioned, is one who loves all of the monotheistic religions and is familiar with their tenets, prefers no one of them above the other. He loves all of humanity. He is a Christian when among Christians, he is a Buddhist when among Buddhists, he is a Taoist when among Taoists, a Zoroastrian when among Zoroastrians, he is a Confucianist when among Confucianists, etc. He knows the slight differences between religions and loves each for its distinct flavor. He knows there is one Universal Religion and that all of the Monotheistic religions together compose the Universal Religion. He understands and knows the Essential Unity of All Religions. He does not seek to bring all religions into one sect or denomination for he understands that diversity and variety are part of God's laws. He has

no prejudice against any of the religions. He is desirous of helping each of them. He is a spiritual individual who has depth,
for he is in truth the instrument of Our Father and the instrument of peace, truth, love and freedom. *Such men should be
consulted.* They seek unity of religions within diversity. *They
know the principles of unity.* They are the truth, the life and the
way. No man can say that he is truthfully educated who has not
grasped a good knowledge of Comparative Religion.   Men like
Abraham Lincoln and Ralph Waldo Emerson were great men because they were men of tremendous spiritual depth and wide
spiritual insight.   THEY SOUGHT THE KINGDOM OF GOD'S
JUSTICE. They knew that faith without good works is hollow.
*Fortunate is the country that possesses such individuals and wise
is the leader who seeks and considers their advice.*

Each problem that leadership faces should be viewed correctly as an opportunity for further growth. Problems are a gift
from God and we should be thankful for the problem and pray
that we find the good solution. *We should thus begin all our
endeavors with the first step, prayer.* We then try to follow the
suggestions mentioned. **We should always consult with those
selected as representatives of the people, their advisors, cabinets,
boards, committees,** etc. We should always keep an open and
receptive mind.

We now come to the next important step: TO TAKE TIME.
There should never be a decision without proper digestion of all
facts and a view of all angles. Premeditation is necessary. No
decision of importance should ever be rushed. Hasty conclusions
are dangerous. We should think before we act. We should not
jump to conclusions. Here is a good story to remember.

Tired and starving, a hunter slogged from the forest where
he had been wandering. His eyes lit up when he spotted a
stranger across the clearing. Throwing down his rifle, he ran to
embrace him.

"THANK HEAVENS!" he cried, "AM I GLAD TO SEE YOU! I'VE BEEN LOST FOR TWO DAYS!"

"WHAT ARE YOU SO GLAD ABOUT?" growled the other man. "I'VE BEEN LOST A WEEK!" (With thanks to The Christophers—N.Y. City)

Before making the decision we should again pray. We pray for divine wisdom and guidance. We should pray with the realization of one's unity with His creator.

After making the decision, we should never have any qualms or misgivings. It is then time to let go and relax. We have done our best and the rest we leave to God. In His hands is the outcome for we realize that we are finite and He is infinite. Let us lose everything in this whole wide world but let us never lose faith. With faith we are bound to progress in our eternal pursuit for a better and happy life and to become stronger men.

It is God's will that the brotherhood of man under the Fatherhood of God become a reality on this earth. HIS KINGDOM WILL COME. IT CAN BE ACHIEVED THROUGH THE SINCERE BROTHERHOOD OF THE MONOTHEISTIC RELIGIONS OF THE WORLD, AND THE SUBSTITUTION OF FORCE WITH RULE BY LAW, THROUGH A SYSTEM OF INTERNATIONAL COURTS, ENFORCED BY A UNITED NATIONS INTERNATIONAL PEACE FORCE.

> "All your strength is your union.
> All your danger is in discord;
> Therefore be at peace henceforward
> And as brothers live together."
>
> Henry Wadsworth Longfellow
> (The son of Hiawatha)

CHAPTER X

The Challenge to Religion
by Eric Butterworth

Religious leaders are engaging today in a continuing dialogue on the question: "What should be the role of religion in this time of turbulent transition in the world?" The answers being offered; ecumenical movements, denominational mergers, modification of ancient doctrines.

One answer that is not often heard: the return to the original concept of "religion"—"to bind together." Ancient religion had no formal doctrine. It was simply a way to strengthen the individual's relationship with God. Prayer was a spontaneous expression of finite man seeking to feel his unity with the infinite It was only as religions became corporate bodies that dogma and ceremony took precedence over the individual quest. In time, the purpose of religion, from the standpoint of its work with the individual, was unity with the Church rather than unity with God.

Ralph Waldo Emerson, in renouncing his role as a clergyman, declared, "Why can not we have a first-hand and immediate experience of God?" He called for a return to the basics of religion, the unitive relationship of the individual with the Infinite. This marked the beginning of a slowly evolving modern religious reformation.

Religious leaders of today would be well-advised to take a new and long look at Paul's speech on Mars Hill as recorded in

Acts 17: ". . . The God that made the world and all things therein, He being the Lord of heaven and earth, dwelleth not in temples made with hands; neither is he served by men's hands, as though He needed anything, seeing He Himself giveth to all life, and breath, and all things . . . that they should seek God, if haply they might feel after Him and find Him, though He is not far from each one of us: for in Him we live and move and have our being."

It is this spiritual relationship that is the key to solving the great needs of the day. Man has simply lost the awareness of his unity with God, with the whole. In his fragmented study of life and of the Universe, he has been unable to see the integrated whole; and it is only in the whole that he can find meaning. Like the "prodigal son" of Jesus' parable, man has been wandering in the "far country," with no strengthening sense of identity or relationship with a "Father" or unifying principle.

Religion contains the answer to the needs of the world today, as it always has; but religion must re-discover itself and its inherent unity principle before it can "save" either man or the world. Scientists freely confess today that they have come to the "edge" of physics, and that only metaphysics can guide them forward. Religion can no longer hold to its credos of past ages. It must gird itself for the role of leadership in the years ahead in the collective formulation of a science of religion and a religion of science.

The day must come when colleges and seminaries will approach the mysteries of life and of the Universe through "new age" courses, such as "the theory of Unitivity." This will outline the basic unity of creation, of sciences, of religions, of mankind. It will emphasize the precedence of points of contact over points of view. It will show the way to peace between men and nations through understanding of the unitive relationship between the finite and the infinite. It will relate in both religious and scientific contexts that man is *not* his brother's keeper, but his brother's brother—that all men exist in the same Infinite Mind, the same eternal Presence.

The religions of the world must achieve a new maturity, putting away the "childish things" of pageantry and performance, and organizing for education and the spiritual development of the individual. The Church should be constantly trying to put itself out of business by developing people who are "within-dependent." Perhaps this is what the Revelator had in mind in his lofty vision of "the city without a church." A startling concept, but the way to the Church's finest hour!

CHAPTER XI

God's Challenge to Mankind

The history of mankind is one where war has been an ever present occurrence. Today man has discovered the use of nuclear weapons, which have the capacity to destroy untold human life, in which event the living will envy the dead. George Bernard Show aptly stated, "Man is intelligent enough to have discovered nuclear fission and damn fool enough to use the nuclear bomb."

In life, there is a duality of nature. There is progression and regression, forward and backward, high and low, evil and good, right and left, life and death, young and old, kindness and cruelty, love and hate, etc. Man has been given freedom of choice and also been endowed with the intelligence to make the right choice.

GOD'S GREAT CHALLENGE TO MANKIND IS TO ELIMINATE WAR. Man is indeed a savage when he resorts to war to settle his disputes. In the final analysis, war settles nothing and always plants the seeds for future wars. Without the elimination of war, man will not be truly civilized nor will he make progress along spiritual lines. Wars can be eliminated; they are not part of life, except through man's foolish choice. How can wars be eliminated? Let us probe the situation.

It is easier to destroy than to build. It is easier to kill than to create or save life. It is easier to hate than to love. It is easier to condemn than to praise. It is easier to be negative than to be positive. It is easier to steal than to create by work. Any man, given a nuclear bomb and the capacity to operate and possess a plane can destroy millions of human beings and tremendous property. Yes, the easy road can bring misery and unhappiness. Is this the destiny of man as a child of God? Man's destiny is to love his neighbor as himself, to treat himself well and also to treat his neighbor equally as well. The elimination of war can be a great adventure and an enjoyable challenge. It will be accomplished. HOW?

The author does not intend to convey any impression that he knows the answers. He is indeed grateful if per chance he knows part of one answer to the problem. With this perspective let us tackle the task diligently.

Our first labor should be the bringing into reality, unity of religions within diversity. Religions must be indicted with the charge that they have failed to be INSTRUMENTS OF PEACE. The prime "raison d'etre" of religions is to bind humanity into one; to foster love for one another; to give mutual aid to each other.

Where one person is suffering so am I. Where one person is starving so am I. Where one person is ill housed so am I. Where one person does not receive spiritual bread so do I. I, in this sense, is not used to denote the writer. The I is used to denote all of us. The I is God. It is the I AM, His name.

The previous chapters of this book attempt to show a path whereby the unity of the monotheistic religions can be achieved. When the First World Conference of Religions is called it should be remembered as "ALL FAITHS' DAY." Every religion should make it a holiday to be remembered through the entire year. The greatest project on earth comes first as a thought, then as words, then as plans followed by action. Creation will result.

When we all pray together we are one. When we all work or play together we are one. This is unity. What has delayed Unity of Religions within Diversity?

THE LOVE AND MISUSE OF POWER, SPIRITUAL EGO-ISM AND FAILURE TO HAVE GOOD LEADERSHIP ARE THE

MAIN REASONS FOR THE PRESENT FAILURE OF RELI-
GIONS TO UNITE. The most important part of the Lord's prayer,
is FOR THINE IS THE KINGDOM, AND THE POWER AND
THE GLORY FOR EVER. Where man loves power, be it in the
realm of religions or nations, we have a violation of God's law.
RELIGIONS MUST ELIMINATE THE QUEST FOR POWER,
THE DOMINATION OF OTHERS. THOSE WHO LOVE POW-
ER ARE NOT FREE. The top step of achievement is TO LOVE
GOD, WITH YOUR WHOLE HEART, BODY AND MIND, AND
TO LOVE YOUR NEIGHBOR AS YOURSELF. Where any group
is powerful it must wisely use this power in the furtherance of
Peace, Love, Truth and Freedom. EGOISM MUST GIVE WAY
TO ALTRUISM. God's laws are always paramount. We take
this universe on HIS terms. We are blessed when we follow His
laws.

All religions must realize that no prophet of any one of the
monotheistic religions has supplanted any other prophet. They
all complement and supplement each other. A truly religious
person does not prefer any one of the monotheistic religions above
the others. He loves them all wholeheartedly and equally as well.
When one shows preference for one religion above the others he
narrows his vision. He needs to study the Essential Unity of all
religions. The greatest harm that can be done by any religion
against another is to emphasize their differences. It is spiritual
immaturity. We should belong to a religion but at the same time
we should love all the others. Faith should have an avenue of
expression.

Let not religions be concerned so much with conflicts between
nations and races. It should be primarily concerned with the
elimination of conflicts between religions. Let us forever remember these immortal words (the truth) enunciated by Dr. Bnagavan
Das in his book "Essential Unity of All Religions":

> "Some persons, disgusted with religious conflict, speak hast-
> ily of abolishing religion to allay that conflict. As well kill

the body to cure disease. To uproot religion successfully, they must first exterminate Pain and Death. So long as human beings experience and fear these, they will not cease to crave the consolations of religion. Also, so long as men and women are left, are encouraged, are even positively taught, to believe that religions differ, even in essentials, so long will they, as followers of such different religions, also necessarily continue to differ, to fight, to shed each other's blood. **If, per contra, they are led to see that all religions are one in essentials, they will also surely become one in heart, and realize their common humanity in a loving Brotherhood."**

When Unity of Religions within diversity is accomplished men will receive the Spiritual Bread that all human beings are entitled to have as their birthright. Man can never live by material bread alone.

In order to achieve peace on this earth, it is necessary that we have RULE BY LAW and not Rule by Force. This can be accomplished by one WORLD GOVERNMENT. The United Nations may, by the grace of God, some day, *mature* into a world government. **All nations must learn, if Peace is to be obtained, that they must sublimate some of their sovereignty to a higher human authority.** International Courts of JUSTICE can then be instituted. The necessary international law codification, practice and procedure to implement and effectuate the rendition of justice and the enforcement of judicial decrees, can be formulated.

A decrease of birth rate is one of mankind's challenge. **The earth's population must be controlled.** As previously mentioned, God did not give his children the right of procreation without the commensurate knowledge and obligation to control sensibly the number of human beings. There is no problem that man faces that is above man's capacity to solve.

In solving the birth rate problem, man should produce food at maximum capacity. It will take time to let people understand the responsibility to decrease the birth rate. In the interim, in order to prevent an explosion of man into another world catastrophe (WAR) all nations that have the wherewithal to step up food production should at once do so. Let us produce foodstuffs to the limit of our capacity and at the same time press to the limit, sensible birth control. Let us ease the tension on both ends. To try to tackle the birth rate problem and fail to increase food production is to aggravate the problem.

The decrease of the death rate, the adequate sheltering and educating of humanity can also be con-current projects, while the solution of the main problem is being achieved. It all means the fulfillment of the great commandment of God—

"LOVE ONE ANOTHER."

THE TEN COMMANDMENTS OF GOD

1. I am the Lord Thy God, thou shalt not have strange gods before Me.

2. Thou shalt not take the name of the Lord Thy God in vain.

3. Remember thou keep holy the Sabbath Day.

4. Honor thy father and thy mother.

5. Thou shalt not kill nor have capital punishment.

6. Thou shalt not commit adultery.

7. Thou shalt not steal.

8. Thou shalt not bear false witness against thy neighbor.

9. Thou shalt not covet thy neighbor's spouse or goods.

10. Thou shalt not exploit, nor be unjust, to others.

(Continued from front flap)

religion has remained dormant. The author points out the way to go.

Amadou Hampate Ba, a great Moslem leader, writer, Ambassador and Statesman, writing to the author stated "How happy I am to hear from the mouth of a Catholic this phrase "Unity of Religions within Diversity. IT DESERVES TO BECOME A SIGN WRITTEN IN LETTERS OF GOLD AND PLACED ABOVE THE DOOR OF EACH HOUSE OF WORSHIP."

No library, place of learning or house of worship is complete without this book. It is a must for every scholar, teacher, preacher and leader. It shows the path that leads to the brotherhood of man.

The author writes with candor and courage. The book stirs the imagination and the intellect. It may well prove to be the most provocative book of our times. The result is a volume that will find a permanent place among the religious writings of the ages.